Na
Pa YO-BVR-522

Allyn
and
Bacon

iSearch:

Criminal Justice

Thomas R. O'Connor
North Carolina Wesleyan

Linda R. Barr
University of the Virgin Islands

Boston | New York | San Francisco
Mexico City | Montreal | Toronto | London | Madrid | Munich | Paris
Hong Kong | Singapore | Tokyo | Cape Town | Sydney

ISBN   0-205-37636-3

Printed in the United States of America

10 9 8 7 6 5 4 3 2 1   08 07 06 05 04 03 02

Contents

iSearch: Criminal Justice

Introduction

Your professor assigns a ten-page research paper that's due in two weeks—and you need to make sure you have up-to-date, credible information. Where do you begin? Today, the easiest answer is the Internet—because it can be so convenient and there is so much information out there. But therein lies part of the problem. How do you know if the information is reliable and from a trustworthy source?

iSearch: Criminal Justice is designed to help you select and evaluate research from the Web to help you find the best and most credible information you can. Throughout this guide, you'll find:

- **A practical and to-the-point discussion of search engines.** Find out which search engines are likely to get you the information you want and how to phrase your searches for the most effective results.
- **Detailed information on evaluating online sources.** Locate credible information on the Web and get tips for thinking critically about Web sites.
- **Citation guidelines for Web resources.** Learn the proper citation guidelines for Web sites, email messages, listservs, and more.
- **Web activities for Criminal Justice.** Explore the various ways you can use the Web in your courses through these online exercises.
- **Web links for Criminal Justice.** Begin your Web research with the discipline-specific sources listed in this section. Also included is information about Web resources offered by Allyn & Bacon—these sites are designed to give you an extra boost in your criminal justice courses.
- **A Quick Guide to ContentSelect.** All you need to know to get started with ContentSelect, a free research database that gives you immediate access to hundreds of scholarly journals and other popular publications, such as *Newsweek*.

So before running straight to your browser, take the time to read through this copy of *iSearch: Criminal Justice* and use it as a reference for all of your Web research needs.

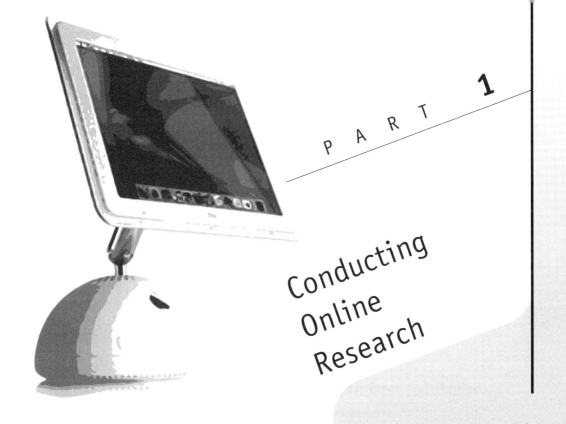

Conducting
Online
Research

Finding Sources:
Search Engines and Subject Directories

Your professor has just given you an assignment to give a five minute speech on the topic "gun control." After a (hopefully brief) panic attack, you begin to think of what type of information you need before you can write the speech. To provide an interesting introduction, you decide to involve your class by taking a straw poll of their views for and against gun control, and to follow this up by giving some statistics on how many Americans favor (and oppose) gun control legislation and then by outlining the arguments on both sides of the issue. If you already know the correct URL for an authoritative Web site like Gallup Opinion Polls (www.gallup.com) or other sites you are in great shape! However, what do you do when you don't have a clue as to which Web site would have information on your topic? In these cases, many, many people routinely (and mistakenly) go to Yahoo! and type in a single term (e.g., guns). This approach is sure to bring first a smile to your face when the results offer you 200,874 hits on your topic, but just as quickly make you grind your teeth in frustration when you start scrolling down the hit list and find sites that range from gun dealerships, to reviews of the video "Young Guns," to aging fan sites for "Guns and Roses."

1

Finding information on a specific topic on the Web is a challenge. The more intricate your research need, the more difficult it is to find the one or two Web sites among the billions that feature the information you want. This section is designed to help you to avoid frustration and to focus in on the right site for your research by using search engines, subject directories, and meta-sites.

Search Engines

Search engines (sometimes called search services) are becoming more numerous on the Web. Originally, they were designed to help users search the Web by topic. More recently, search engines have added features which enhance their usefulness, such as searching a particular part of the Web (e.g., only sites of educational institutions—dot.edu), retrieving just one site which the search engine touts as most relevant (like Ask Jeeves {www.aj.com}), or retrieving up to 10 sites which the search engine rank as most relevant (like Google {www.google.com}).

Search Engine Defined

According to Cohen (1999):

> "A search engine service provides a searchable database of Internet files collected by a computer program called a wanderer, crawler, robot, worm, or spider. Indexing is created from the collected files, and the results are presented in a schematic order. There are no selection criteria for the collection of files.
>
> A search service therefore consists of three components: (1) a spider, a program that traverses the Web from link to link, identifying and reading pages; (2) an index, a database containing a copy of each Web page gathered by the spider; and (3) a search engine mechanism, software that enables users to query the index and then returns results in a schematic order (p. 31)."

One problem students often have in their use of search engines is that they are deceptively easy to use. Like our example "guns," no matter what is typed into the handy box at the top, links to numerous Web sites appear instantaneously, lulling students into a false sense of security. Since so much was retrieved, surely SOME of it must be useful. WRONG! Many Web sites retrieved will be very light on substantive content, which is not what you need for most academic endeavors. Finding just the right Web site has been likened to finding diamonds in the desert.

As you can see by the definition above, one reason for this is that most search engines use indexes developed by machines. Therefore they are indexing terms not concepts. The search engine cannot tell the difference between the keyword "crack" to mean a split in the sidewalk and "crack" referring to crack cocaine. To use search engines properly takes some skill, and this chapter will provide tips to help you use search engines more effectively. First, however, let's look at the different types of search engines with examples:

TYPES OF SEARCH ENGINES		
TYPE	DESCRIPTION	EXAMPLES
1st Generation	• Non-evaluative, do not evaluate results in terms of content or authority. • Return results ranked by relevancy alone (number of times the term(s) entered appear, usually on the first paragraph or page of the site)	AltaVista (www.altavista.com/) Excite (www.excite.com) HotBot (www.HotBot.com) Infoseek (guide.infoseek.com) Ixquick Metasearch (ixquick.com) Lycos (www.lycos.com)
2nd Generation	• More creative in displaying results. • Results are ordered by characteristics such as: concept, document type, Web site, popularity, etc. rather than relevancy.	Ask Jeeves (www.aj.com/) Direct Hit (www.directhit.com/) Google! (www.google.com/) HotLinks (www.hotlinks.com/) Simplifind (www.simpli.com/) SurfWax (www.surfwax.com/) Also see Meta-Search engines below. EVALUATIVE SEARCH ENGINES About.Com (www.about.com) WebCrawler (www.webcrawler.com)
Commercial Portals	• Provide additional features such as: customized news, stock quotations, weather reports, shopping, etc. • They want to be used as a "one stop" Web guide. • They profit from prominent advertisements and fees charged to featured sites.	GONetwork (www.go.com/) Google Web Directory (directory.google.com/) LookSmart (www.looksmart.com/) My Starting Point (www.stpt.com/) Open Directory Project (dmoz.org/) NetNow (www.inetnow.com) Yahoo! (www.yahoo.com/)
Meta-Search Engines	Run searches on multiple search engines.	There are different types of meta-search engines. See the next 2 boxes.

(continued)

TYPES OF SEARCH ENGINES, *continued*		
TYPE	DESCRIPTION	EXAMPLES
Meta-Search Engines *Integrated Result*	• Display results for search engines in one list. • Duplicates are removed. • Only portions of results from each engine are returned.	Beaucoup.com (www.beaucoup.com/) Highway 61 (www.highway61.com) Cyber411(www.cyber411. com/) Mamma (www.mamma.com/) MetaCrawler (www. metacrawler.com/) Visisimo (www.vivisimo.com) Northern Light (www.nlsearch.com/) SurfWax (www.surfwax.com)
Meta-Search Engines *Non-Integrated Results*	• Comprehensive search. • Displays results from each search engine in separate results sets. • Duplicates remain. • You must sift through all the sites.	Dogpile (www.dogpile.com) Global Federated Search (jin.dis.vt.edu/fedsearch/) GoHip (www.gohip.com) Searchalot (www.searchalot.com) 1Blink (www.1blink.com) ProFusion (www. profusion.com/)

QUICK TIPS FOR MORE EFFECTIVE USE OF SEARCH ENGINES

1. Use a search engine:
   • When you have a narrow idea to search.
   • When you want to search the full text of countless Web pages
   • When you want to retrieve a large number of sites
   • When the features of the search engine (like searching particular parts of the Web) help with your search

2. Always use Boolean Operators to combine terms. Searching on a single term is a sure way to retrieve a very large number of Web pages, few, if any, of which are on target.
   • Always check search engine's HELP feature to see what symbols are used for the operators as these vary (e.g., some engines use the & or + symbol for AND).
   • Boolean Operators include:
     AND to narrow search and to make sure that **both** terms are included
       e.g:, children AND violence
     OR to broaden search and to make sure that **either** term is included
       e.g., child OR children OR juveniles
     NOT to **exclude** one term
       e.g., eclipse NOT lunar

iSearch: Criminal Justice

3. Use appropriate symbols to indicate important terms and to indicate phrases (Best Bet for Constructing a Search According to Cohen (1999): Use a plus sign (+) in front of terms you want to retrieve: +solar +eclipse. Place a phrase in double quotation marks: "solar eclipse" Put together: "+solar eclipse" "+South America").

4. Use word stemming (a.k.a. truncation) to find all variations of a word (check search engine HELP for symbols).
   - If you want to retrieve child, child's, or children use child* (some engines use other symbols such as !, #, or $)
   - Some engines automatically search singular and plural terms, check HELP to see if yours does.

5. Since search engines only search a portion of the Web, use several search engines or a meta-search engine to extend your reach.

6. Remember search engines are generally mindless drones that do not evaluate. Do not rely on them to find the best Web sites on your topic, use *subject directories* or meta-sites to enhance value (see below).

Finding Those Diamonds in the Desert: Using Subject Directories and Meta-sites

Although some search engines, like WebCrawler (www.webcrawler.com) do evaluate the Web sites they index, most search engines do not make any judgment on the worth of the content. They just return a long—sometimes very long—list of sites that contained your keyword. However, *subject directories* exist that are developed by human indexers, usually librarians or subject experts, and are defined by Cohen (1999) as follows:

> "A subject directory is a service that offers a collection of links to Internet resources submitted by site creators or evaluators and organized into subject categories. Directory services use selection criteria for choosing links to include, though the selectivity varies among services (p. 27)."

World Wide Web Subject directories are useful when you want to see sites on your topic that have been reviewed, evaluated, and selected for their authority, accuracy, and value. They can be real time savers for students, since subject directories weed out the commercial, lightweight, or biased Web sites.

Metasites are similar to subject directories, but are more specific in nature, usually dealing with one scholarly field or discipline. Some examples of subject directories and meta-sites are found in the table on the next page.

Choose subject directories to ensure that you are searching the highest quality Web pages. As an added bonus, subject directories periodically check Web links to make sure that there are fewer dead ends and out-dated links.

iSearch: Criminal Justice

SMART SEARCHING—SUBJECT DIRECTORIES AND META-SITES	
TYPES—SUBJECT DIRECTORIES	EXAMPLES
General, covers many topics	Access to Internet and Subject Resources (www2.lib.udel.edu/subj/)
	Best Information on the Net (BIOTN) (http://library.sau.edu/bestinfo/)
	Federal Web Locator (www.infoctr.edu/fwl/)
	Galaxy (galaxy.einet.net)
	INFOMINE: Scholarly Internet Resource Collections (infomine.ucr.edu/)
	InfoSurf: Resources by Subject (www.library.ucsb.edu/subj/)
	Librarian's Index to the Internet (www.lii.org/)
	Martindale's "The Reference Desk" (www-sci.lib.uci.edu/HSG/ref.html)
	PINAKES: A Subject Launchpad (www.hw.ac.uk/libWWW/irn/pinakes/pinakes.html)
	Refdesk.com (www.refdesk.com)
	Search Engines and Subject Directories (College of New Jersey) (www.tcnj.edu/~library/research/internet_search.html)
	Scout Report Archives (www.scout.cs.wisc.edu/archives)
	Selected Reference Sites (www.mnsfld.edu/depts/lib/mu~ref.html)
	WWW Virtual Library (http://vlib.org)
Subject Oriented	
• Communication Studies	The Media and Communication Studies Site (www.aber.ac.uk/media)
	University of Iowa Department of Communication Studies (www.uiowa.edu/~commstud/resources)
• Cultural Studies	Sara Zupko's Cultural Studies Center (www.popcultures.com)
• Education	Educational Virtual Library (www.csu.edu.au/education/library.html)
	ERIC [Education ResourcesInformation Center] (ericir.sunsite.syr.edu/)
	Kathy Schrock's Guide for Educators (kathyschrock.net/abceval/index.htm)
• Journalism	Journalism Resources (bailiwick.lib.uiowa.edu/journalism/)
	Journalism and Media Criticism page (www.chss.montclair.edu/english/furr/media.html)
• Literature	Norton Web Source to American Literature (www.wwnorton.com/naal)
	Project Gutenberg [Over 3,000 full text titles] (www.gutenberg.net)

SMART SEARCHING, *continued*	
TYPES—SUBJECT DIRECTORIES	EXAMPLES
• Medicine & Health	PubMed [National Library of Medicine's index to Medical Journals, 1966 to present] (www.ncbi.nlm.nih.gov/PubMed/) RxList: The Internet Drug Index (rxlist.com) Go Ask Alice (www.goaskalice.columbia.edu) [Health and sexuality]
• Technology	CNET.com (www.cnet.com)

Another closely related group of sites are the *Virtual Library sites,* also referred to as Digital Library sites. Hopefully, your campus library has an outstanding Web site for both on-campus and off-campus access to resources. If not, there are several virtual library sites that you can use, although you should realize that some of the resources would be subscription based, and not accessible unless you are a student of that particular university or college. These are useful because, like the subject directories and meta-sites, experts have organized Web sites by topic and selected only those of highest quality.

You now know how to search for information and use search engines more effectively. In the next section, you will learn more tips for evaluating the information that you found.

VIRTUAL LIBRARY SITES	
PUBLIC LIBRARIES	
• Internet Public Library	www.ipl.org
• Library of Congress	lcweb.loc.gov/homepage/lchp.html
• New York Public Library	www.nypl.org
University/College Libraries	
• Bucknell	jade.bucknell.edu/
• Case Western	www.cwru.edu/uclibraries.html
• Dartmouth	www.dartmouth.edu/~library
• Duke	www.lib.duke.edu/
• Franklin & Marshall	www.library.fandm.edu
• Harvard	www.harvard.edu/museums/
• Penn State	www.libraries.psu.edu
• Princeton	infoshare1.princeton.edu
• Stanford	www.slac.stanford.edu/FIND/spires.html
• ULCA	www.library.ucla.edu

(continued)

iSearch: Criminal Justice

iSearch: Criminal Justice

VIRTUAL LIBRARY SITES, *continued*

PUBLIC LIBRARIES

Other
• Perseus Project [subject specific—classics, supported by   www.perseus.tufts.edu
  grants from corporations and educational institutions]

BIBLIOGRAPHY FOR FURTHER READING

Books

Basch, Reva. (1996). Secrets of the Super Net Searchers.

Berkman, Robert I. (2000). *Find It Fast: How to Uncover Expert Information on Any Subject Online or in Print.* NY: HarperResource.

Glossbrenner, Alfred & Glossbrenner, Emily. (1999). *Search Engines for the World Wide Web,* 2nd Ed. Berkeley, CA: Peachpit Press.

Hock, Randolph, & Berinstein, Paula.. (1999). *The Extreme Searcher's Guide to Web Search Engines: A Handbook for the Serious Searcher.* Information Today, Inc.

Miller, Michael. *Complete Idiot's Guide to Yahoo!* (2000). Indianapolis, IN: Que.

Miller, Michael. *Complete Idiot's Guide to Online Search Secrets.* (2000). Indianapolis, IN: Que.

Paul, Nora, Williams, Margot, & Hane, Paula. (1999). *Great Scouts!: CyberGuides for Subject Searching on the Web.* Information Today, Inc.

Radford, Marie, Barnes, Susan, & Barr, Linda (2001). *Web Research: Selecting, Evaluating, and Citing* Boston. Allyn and Bacon.

Journal Articles

Cohen, Laura B. (1999, August). The Web as a research tool: Teaching strategies for instructors. *CHOICE Supplement 3,* 20–44.

Cohen, Laura B. (August 2000). Searching the Web: The Human Element Emerges. *CHOICE Supplement 37,* 17–31.

Introna, Lucas D., & Nissenbaum, Helen. (2000). Shaping the web: Why the politics of search engines matters. The Information Society, Vol. 16, No. 3, pp. 169–185.

Evaluating Sources on the Web

Congratulations! You've found a great Web site. Now what? The Web site you found seems like the perfect Web site for your research. But, are you sure? Why is it perfect? What criteria are you using to determine whether this Web site suits your purpose?

Think about it. Where else on earth can anyone "publish" information regardless of the *accuracy, currency,* or *reliability* of the information? The

Internet has opened up a world of opportunity for posting and distributing information and ideas to virtually everyone, even those who might post misinformation for fun, or those with ulterior motives for promoting their point of view. Armed with the information provided in this guide, you can dig through the vast amount of useless information and misinformation on the World Wide Web to uncover the valuable information. Because practically anyone can post and distribute their ideas on the Web, you need to develop a new set of *critical thinking skills* that focus on the evaluation of the quality of information, rather than be influenced and manipulated by slick graphics and flashy moving java script.

Before the existence of online sources, the validity and accuracy of a source was more easily determined. For example, in order for a book to get to the publishing stage, it must go through many critiques, validation of facts, reviews, editorial changes and the like. Ownership of the information in the book is clear because the author's name is attached to it. The publisher's reputation is on the line too. If the book turns out to have incorrect information, reputations and money can be lost. In addition, books available in a university library are further reviewed by professional librarians and selected for library purchase because of their accuracy and value to students. Journal articles downloaded or printed from online subscription services, such as Infotrac, ProQuest, EbscoHost, or other fulltext databases, are put through the same scrutiny as the paper versions of the journals.

On the World Wide Web, however, Internet service providers (ISPs) simply give Web site authors a place to store information. The Web site author can post information that may not be validated or tested for accuracy. One mistake students typically make is to assume that all information on the Web is of equal value. Also, in the rush to get assignments in on time, students may not take the extra time to make sure that the information they are citing is accurate. It is easy just to cut and paste without really thinking about the content in a critical way. However, to make sure you are gathering accurate information and to get the best grade on your assignments, it is vital that you develop your critical ability to sift through the dirt to find the diamonds.

Web Evaluation Criteria

So, here you are, at this potentially great site. Let's go though some ways you can determine if this site is one you can cite with confidence in your research. Keep in mind, ease of use of a Web site is an issue, but more important is learning how to determine the validity of data, facts, and statements for your use. The five traditional ways to verify a paper source can also be applied to your Web source: *accuracy, authority, objectivity, coverage,* and *currency.*

Evaluating Web Sites Using
Five Criteria to Judge Web Site Content

Accuracy—How reliable is the information?

Authority—Who is the author and what are his or her credentials?

Objectivity—Does the Web site present a balanced or biased point of view?

Coverage—Is the information comprehensive enough for your needs?

Currency—Is the Web site up to date?

Use additional criteria to judge Web site content, including

- **Publisher, documentation, relevance, scope, audience, appropriateness of format,** and **navigation**
- Judging whether the site is made up of **primary (original) or secondary (interpretive) sources**
- Determining whether the information is **relevant** to your research

Content Evaluation

Accuracy.   Internet searches are not the same as searches of library databases because much of the information on the Web has not been edited, whereas information in databases has. It is your responsibility to make sure that the information you use in a school project is accurate. When you examine the content on a Web site or Web page, you can ask yourself a number of questions to determine whether the information is accurate.

1. Is the information reliable?
2. Do the facts from your other research contradict the facts you find on this Web page?
3. Do any misspellings and/or grammar mistakes indicate a hastily put together Web site that has not been checked for accuracy?
4. Is the content on the page verifiable through some other source? Can you find similar facts elsewhere (journals, books, or other online sources) to support the facts you see on this Web page?
5. Do you find links to other Web sites on a similar topic? If so, check those links to ascertain whether they back up the information you see on the Web page you are interested in using.
6. Is a bibliography of additional sources for research provided? Lack of a bibliography doesn't mean the page isn't accurate, but having one allows you further investigation points to check the information.
7. Does the site of a research document or study explain how the data was collected and the type of research method used to interpret the data?

iSearch: Criminal Justice

If you've found a site with information that seems too good to be true, it may be. You need to verify information that you read on the Web by cross-checking against other sources.

Authority.   An important question to ask when you are evaluating a Web site is, "Who is the author of the information?" Do you know whether the author is a recognized authority in his or her field? Biographical information, references to publications, degrees, qualifications, and organizational affiliations can help to indicate an author's authority. For example, if you are researching the topic of laser surgery citing a medical doctor would be better than citing a college student who has had laser surgery.

The organization sponsoring the site can also provide clues about whether the information is fact or opinion. Examine how the information was gathered and the research method used to prepare the study or report. Other questions to ask include:

1. Who is responsible for the content of the page? Although a webmaster's name is often listed, this person is not necessarily responsible for the content.
2. Is the author recognized in the subject area? Does this person cite any other publications he or she has authored?
3. Does the author list his or her background or credentials (e.g., Ph.D. degree, title such as professor, or other honorary or social distinction)?
4. Is there a way to contact the author? Does the author provide a phone number or email address?
5. If the page is mounted by an organization, is it a known, reputable one?
6. How long has the organization been in existence?
7. Does the URL for the Web page end in the extension .edu or .org? Such extensions indicate authority compared to dotcoms (.com), which are commercial enterprises. (For example, www.cancer.com takes you to an online drugstore that has a cancer information page; www.cancer.org is the American Cancer Society Web site.)

A good idea is to ask yourself whether the author or organization presenting the information on the Web is an authority on the subject. If the answer is no, this may not be a good source of information.

Objectivity.   Every author has a point of view, and some views are more controversial than others. Journalists try to be objective by providing both sides of a story. Academics attempt to persuade readers by presenting a logical argument, which cites other scholars' work. You need to look for two sided arguments in news and information sites. For academic papers, you need to determine how the paper fits within its discipline and whether the author is using controversial methods for reporting a conclusion.

Authoritative authors situate their work within a larger discipline. This background helps readers evaluate the author's knowledge on a particular

iSearch: Criminal Justice

subject. You should ascertain whether the author's approach is controversial and whether he or she acknowledges this. More important, is the information being presented as fact or opinion? Authors who argue for their position provide readers with other sources that support their arguments. If no sources are cited, the material may be an opinion piece rather than an objective presentation of information. The following questions can help you determine objectivity:

1. Is the purpose of the site clearly stated, either by the author or the organization authoring the site?
2. Does the site give a balanced viewpoint or present only one side?
3. Is the information directed toward a specific group of viewers?
4. Does the site contain advertising?
5. Does the copyright belong to a person or an organization?
6. Do you see anything to indicate who is funding the site?

Everyone has a point of view. This is important to remember when you are using Web resources. A question to keep asking yourself is, What is the bias or point of *view* being expressed here?

Coverage.   Coverage deals with the breadth and depth of information presented on a Web site. Stated another way, it is about how much information is presented and how detailed the information is. Looking at the site map or index can give you an idea about how much information is contained on a site. This isn't necessarily bad. Coverage is a criteria that is tied closely to *your* research requirement. For one assignment, a given Web site may be too general for your needs. For another assignment, that same site might be perfect. Some sites contain very little actual information because pages are filled with links to other sites. Coverage also relates to objectivity You should ask the following questions about coverage:

1. Does the author present both sides of the story or is a piece of the story missing?
2. Is the information comprehensive enough for your needs?
3. Does the site cover too much, too generally?
4. Do you need more specific information than the site can provide?
5. Does the site have an objective approach?

In addition to examining what is covered on a Web site, equally revealing is what is not covered. Missing information can reveal a bias in the material. Keep in mind that you are evaluating the information on a Web site for your research requirements.

Currency.   Currency questions deal with the timeliness of information. However, currency is more important for some topics than for others. For example, currency is essential when you are looking for technology related topics and current events. In contrast, currency may not be relevant when you are doing research on Plato or Ancient Greece. In terms of Web sites, currency also pertains to whether the site is being kept up to date and links are being maintained. Sites on the Web are sometimes abandoned by their owners. When people move or change jobs, they may neglect to remove theft site from the company or university server. To test currency ask the following questions:

1. Does the site indicate when the content was created?
2. Does the site contain a last revised date? How old is the date? (In the early part of 2001, a university updated their Web site with a "last up-dated" date of 1901! This obviously was a Y2K problem, but it does point out the need to be observant of such things!)
3. Does the author state how often he or she revises the information? Some sites are on a monthly update cycle (e.g., a government statistics page).
4. Can you tell specifically what content was revised?
5. Is the information still useful for your topic? Even if the last update is old, the site might still be worthy of use *if* the content is still valid for your research.

Relevancy to Your Research: Primary versus Secondary Sources

Some research assignments require the use of primary (original) sources. Materials such as raw data, diaries, letters, manuscripts, and original accounts of events can be considered primary material. In most cases, these historical documents are no longer copyrighted. The Web is a great source for this type of resource.

Information that has been analyzed and previously interpreted is considered a secondary source. Sometimes secondary sources are more appropriate than primary sources. If, for example, you are asked to analyze a topic or to find an analysis of a topic, a secondary source of an analysis would be most appropriate. Ask yourself the following questions to determine whether the Web site is relevant to your research:

1. Is it a primary or secondary source?
2. Do you need a primary source?
3. Does the assignment require you to cite different types of sources? For example, are you supposed to use at least one book, one journal article, and one Web page?

You need to think critically, both visually and verbally, when evaluating Web sites. Because Web sites are designed as multimedia hypertexts, nonlinear texts, visual elements, and navigational tools are added to the evaluation process.

iSearch: Criminal Justice

Help in Evaluating Web Sites.   One shortcut to finding high-quality Web sites is using subject directories and meta-sites, which select the Web sites they index by similar evaluation criteria to those just described. If you want to learn more about evaluating Web sites, many colleges and universities provide sites that help you evaluate Web resources. The following list contains some excellent examples of these evaluation sites:

- Evaluating Quality on the Net—Hope Tillman, Babson College
  www.hopetillman.com/findqual.html
- Critical Web Evaluation—Kurt W. Wagner, William Paterson University of New Jersey
  euphrates.wpunj.edu/faculty/wagnerk/
- Evalation Criteria—Susan Beck, New Mexico State University
  lib.nmsu.edu/instruction/evalcrit.html
- A Student's Guide to Research with the WWW
  www.slu.edu/departments/english/research/
- Evaluating Web Pages: Questions to Ask & Strategies for Getting the Answers
  www.lib.berkeley.edu/TeachingLib/Guides/Internet/
  EvalQuestions.html

Critical Evaluation Web Sites

WEB SITE AND URL	SOURCE
Critical Thinking in an Online World **www.library.ucsb.edu/untangle/ jones.html**	*Paper from "Untangling the Web" 1996*
Educom Review: Information **www.educause.edu/pub/er/review/ reviewArticles/31231.html**	*EDUCAUSE Literacy as a Liberal Art (1996 article)*
Evaluating Information Found on the Internet **MiltonsWeb.mse.jhu.edu/ research/education/net.html**	*University of Utah Library*
Evaluating Web Sites **www.lib.purdue.edu/InternetEval**	*Purdue University Library*
Evaluating Web Sites **www.lehigh.edu/~inref/guides/ evaluating.web.html**	*Lehigh University*
ICONnect: Curriculum Connections Overview **www.ala.org/ICONN/evaluate.html**	*American Library Association's technology education initiative*
Kathy Schrock's ABC's of Web Site Evaluation **www.kathyschrock.net/abceval/**	*Author's Web site*

Kids Pick the best of the Web
"Top 10: Announced"
www.ala.org/news/topkidpicks.html

*American Library Association
initiative underwritten by
Microsoft (1998)*

Resource Selection and Information
Evaluation
**alexia.lis.uiuc.edu/~janicke/
InfoAge.html**

*Univ of Illinois, Champaign-
Urbana (Librarian)*

Testing the Surf: Criteria for Evaluating
Internet Information Sources
**info.lib.uh.edu/pr/v8/n3/
smit8n3.html**

University of Houston Libraries

Evaluating Web Resources
**www2.widener.edu/
Wolfgram-Memorial-Library/
webevaluation/webeval.htm**

Widener University Library

UCLA College Library Instruction:
Thinking Critically about World
Wide Web Resources
**www.library.ucla.edu/libraries/
college/help/critical/**

UCLA Library

UG OOL: Judging Quality on the Internet
**www.open.uoguelph.ca/resources/
skills/judging.html**

University of Guelph

Web Evaluation Criteria
**lib.nmsu.edu/instruction/
evalcrit.html**

*New Mexico State University
Library*

Web Page Credibility Checklist
**www.park.pvt.k12.md.us/academics/
research/credcheck.htm**

Park School of Baltimore

Evaluating Web Sites for Educational
Uses: Bibliography and Checklist
www.unc.edu/cit/guides/irg-49.html

University of North Carolina

Evaluating Web Sites
**www.lesley.edu/library/guides/
research/evaluating_web.html**

Lesley University

> *Tip:* Can't seem to get a URL to work? If the URL doesn't begin with www,
> you may need to put the http:// in front of the URL. Usually, browsers can
> handle URLs that begin with www without the need to type in the "http://"
> but if you find you're having trouble, add the http://.

Documentation Guidelines for Online Sources

Your Citation for Exemplary Research

There's another detail left for us to handle—the formal citing of electronic sources in academic papers. The very factor that makes research on the Internet exciting is the same factor that makes referencing these sources challenging: their dynamic nature. A journal article exists, either in print or on microfilm, virtually forever. A document on the Internet can come, go, and change without warning. Because the purpose of citing sources is to allow another scholar to retrace your argument, a good citation allows a reader to obtain information from your primary sources, to the extent possible. This means you need to include not only information on when a source was posted on the Internet (if available) but also when you obtained the information.

The two arbiters of form for academic and scholarly writing are the Modern Language Association (MLA) and the American Psychological Association (APA); both organizations have established styles for citing electronic publications.

MLA Style

In the fifth edition of the *MLA Handbook for Writers of Research Papers,* the MLA recommends the following formats:

- **URLs:** URLs are enclosed in angle brackets (<>) and contain the access mode identifier, the formal name for such indicators as "http" or "ftp." If a URL must be split across two lines, break it only after a slash (/). Never introduce a hyphen at the end of the first line. The URL should include all the parts necessary to identify uniquely the file/document being cited.

  <http://www.csun.edu/~rtvfdept/home/index.html>

- **An online scholarly project or reference database:** A complete "online reference contains the title of the project or database (underlined); the name of the editor of the project or database (if given); electronic publication information, including version number (if relevant and if not part of the title), date of electronic publication or latest update, and name of any sponsoring institution or organization; date of access; and electronic address.

The Perseus Project. Ed. Gregory R. Crane. Mar. 1997. Department of Classics, Tufts University. 15 June 1998 <http://www.perseus.tufts.edu/>.

If you cannot find some of the information, then include the information that is available. The MLA also recommends that you print or download electronic documents, freezing them in time for future reference.

- **A document within a scholarly project or reference database:** It is much more common to use only a portion of a scholarly project or database. To cite an essay, poem, or other short work, begin this citation with the name of the author and the title of the work (in quotation marks). Then, include all the information used when citing a complete online scholarly project or reference database, however, make sure you use the URL of the specific work and not the address of the general site.

Cuthberg, Lori. "Moonwalk: Earthlings' Finest Hour."
     <u>Discovery Channel Online</u>. 1999. Discovery
     Channel. 25 Nov. 1999 <http://www.discovery.com/
     indep/newsfeatures/moonwalk/challenge.html>.

- **A professional or personal site:** Include the name of the person creating the site (reversed), followed by a period, the title of the site (underlined), or, if there is no title, a description such as Home page (such a description is neither placed in quotes nor underlined). Then, specify the name of any school, organization, or other institution affiliated with the site and follow it with your date of access and the URL of the page.

Packer, Andy. Home page. 1Apr. 1998 <http://
     www.suu.edu/~students/Packer.htm>.

Some electronic references are truly unique to the online domain. These include email, newsgroup postings, MUDs (multiuser domains) or MOOs (multiuser domains, object-oriented), and IRCs (Internet Relay Chats).

Email. In citing email messages, begin with the writer's name (reversed) followed by a period, then the title of the message (if any) in quotations as it appears in the subject line. Next comes a description of the message, typically "Email to," and the recipient (e.g., "the author"), and finally the date of the message.

Davis, Jeffrey. "Web Writing Resources." Email to
     Nora Davis. 3 Jan. 2000.

Sommers, Laurice. "Re: College Admissions
     Practices." Email to the author. 12 Aug. 1998.

iSearch: Criminal Justice

List Servers and Newsgroups.   In citing these references, begin with the author's name (reversed) followed by a period. Next include the title of the document (in quotes) from the subject line, followed by the words "Online posting" (not in quotes). Follow this with the date of posting. For list servers, include the date of access, the name of the list (if known), and the online address of the list's moderator or administrator. For newsgroups, follow "Online posting" with the date of posting, the date of access, and the name of the newsgroup, prefixed with "news:" and enclosed in angle brackets.

```
Applebaum, Dale. "Educational Variables." Online
    posting. 29 Jan. 1998. Higher Education
    Discussion Group. 30 Jan. 1993
    <jlucidoj@unc.edu>.
```

```
Gostl, Jack. "Re: Mr. Levitan." Online posting.
    13 June 1997. 20 June 1997
    <news:alt.edu.bronxscience>.
```

MUDs, MOOs, and IRCs.   Begin with the name of the speaker(s) followed by a period. Follow with the description and date of the event, the forum in which the communication took place, the date of access, and the online address. If you accessed the MOO or MUD through telnet, your citation might appear as follows:

```
Guest. Personal interview. 13 Aug. 1998.
    <telnet://du.edu:8888>.
```

For more information on MLA documentation style for online sources, check out their Web site at http://www.mla.org/style/sources.htm.

APA Style

The newly revised *Publication Manual of the American Psychological Association* (5th ed.) now includes guidelines for Internet resources. The manual recommends that, at a minimum, a reference of an Internet source should provide a document title or description, a date (either the date of publication or update or the date of retrieval), and an address (in Internet terms, a uniform resource locator, or URL). Whenever possible, identify the authors of a document as well. It's important to remember that, unlike the MLA, the APA does not include temporary or transient sources (e.g., letters, phone calls, etc.) in its "References" page, preferring to handle them in the text. The general suggested format is as follows:

Online periodical:

Author, A. A., Author, B. B., & Author, C. C.
    (2000). Title of article. *Title of Periodical,*
    xx, xxxxx. Retrieved month, day, year, from
    source.

Online document:

Author, A. A. (2000). *Title of work.* Retrieved
    month, day, year, from source.

Some more specific examples are as follows:

FTP (File Transfer Protocol) Sites. To cite files available for downloading via FTP, give the author's name (if known), the publication date (if available and if different from the date accessed), the full title of the paper (capitalizing only the first word and proper nouns), the date of access, and the address of the FTP site along with the full path necessary to access the file.

Deutsch, P. (1991) Archie: An electronic directory
    service for the Internet. Retrieved January 25,
    2000 from File Transfer Protocol: ftp://
    ftp.sura.net/pub/archie/docs/whatis.archie

WWW Sites (World Wide Web). To cite files available for viewing or downloading via the World Wide Web, give the author's name (if known), the year of publication (if known and if different from the date accessed), the full title of the article, and the title of the complete work (if applicable) in italics. Include any additional information (such as versions, editions, or revisions) in parentheses immediately following the title. Include the date of retrieval and full URL (the http address).

Burka, L. P. (1993). A hypertext history of multi-
    user dungeons. *MUDdex.* Retrieved January 13, 1997
    from the World Wide Web: http://www.utopia.com/
    talent/lpb/muddex/essay/

Tilton, J. (1995). Composing good HTML (Vers. 2.0.6).
    Retrieved December 1, 1996 from the World Wide Web:
    http://www.cs.cmu.edu/~tilt/cgh/

Synchronous Communications (MOOs, MUDs, IRC, etc.). Give the name of the speaker(s), the complete date of the conversation being referenced in parentheses, and the title of the session (if applicable). Next, list the title of the site in italics, the protocol and address (if applicable), and any directions necessary to access the work. Last, list the date of access, followed by the retrieval information. Personal interviews do not need to be listed in the References, but do need to be included in parenthetic references in the text (see the APA *Publication Manual*).

Cross, J. (1996, February 27). Netoric's Tuesday
    "cafe: Why use MUDs in the writing classroom?
    MediaMoo. Retrieved March 1, 1996 from File
    Transfer Protocol: ftp://daedalus.com/
    pub/ACW/NETORIC/catalog

Gopher Sites.   List the author's name (if applicable), the year of publication, the title of the file or paper, and the title of the complete work (if applicable). Include any print publication information (if available) followed by the protocol (i.e., gopher://). List the date that the file was accessed and the path necessary to access the file.

Massachusetts Higher Education Coordinating Council.
    (1994). Using coordination and collaboration to
    address change. Retrieved July 16, 1999 from the
    World Wide Web: gopher://gopher.mass.edu:170/
    00gopher_root%3A%5B_hecc%5D_plan

Email, Listservs, and Newsgroups.   Do not include personal email in the list of References. Although unretrievable communication such as email is not included in APA References, somewhat more public or accessible Internet postings from newsgroups or listservs may be included. See the APA *Publication Manual* for information on in-text citations.

Heilke, J. (1996, May 3). Webfolios. Alliance for
    Computers and Writing Discussion List. Retrieved
    December 31, 1996 from the World Wide Web:
    http://www.ttu.edu/lists/acw-l/9605/0040.html

Other authors and educators have proposed similar extensions to the APA style. You can find links to these pages at:

www.psychwww.com/resource/apacrib.htm

Remember, "frequently-referenced" does not equate to "correct" "or even "desirable." Check with your professor to see if your course or school has a preference for an extended APA style.

iSearch: Criminal Justice

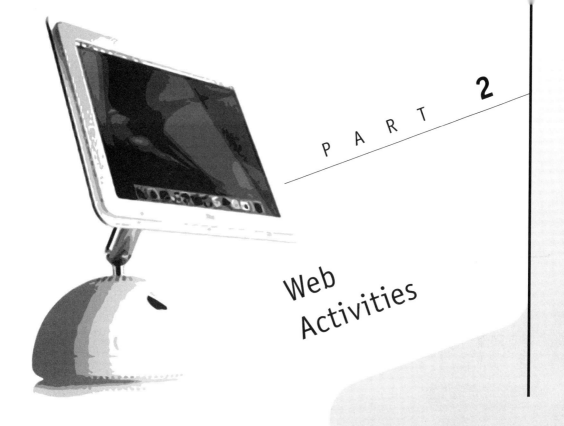

Web
Activities

Internet Activities for Criminology and Criminal Justice

In Part I we examined the variety of ways that the Internet has been used in criminology and criminal justice. We looked at comprehensive Web sites, specialized sites, research sites, law sites, agency sites, and job sites. This does not begin, however, to exhaust the endless possibilities for what the Internet can provide in the hands of a skillful Web surfer. In this section, therefore, we have prepared a series of activities to help you fine-tune your abilities at using the Internet in criminology and criminal justice.

Let's assume you are just beginning your career in criminology and criminal justice; that is, you're close to graduation and you want to start looking at ways to ply your trade or set up shop. Let's also assume you're interested in applying what you've learned in college, like the abilities to analyze crime, understand criminal offenders, and know how the criminal justice system is supposed to operate.

Think of these exercises, then, as routes or stages to a more productive and satisfying professional career. In fact, they do represent how a professional in criminology and criminal justice would use the Internet.

Specifically, we will look at how you can use the Internet to accomplish the following objectives:

- Scan the latest crime news and headlines
- Review relevant criminological theories
- Check out what the think tanks think
- Agree or disagree with the ACLU
- Evaluate professional associations and their journals
- Get government grant money
- Take a stand on a crime bill
- Look for a better job

Scan the Latest Crime News and Headlines

One of the great benefits of the Internet is news gathering. You can literally read tomorrow's online edition of the news before the printed version hits the newsstands. Not only are there many excellent Internet sources for crime news, some sources even index the crime news from all the nation's newspapers for you.

1. Start your browser and go to **http://www.apbonline.com/**
2. Note how the Web site is organized. See if there are discussion forums, mailing lists, or chat rooms of interest to you, but focus on the crime stories and late-breaking news.
3. Go ahead and click on a few of the crime stories.

   Name two or three of the newspapers or other sources which apbonline.com relies upon in getting their stories.

   _____

   _____

   _____

   What types of crime does it seem that apbonline.com covers?

   _____

   _____

   _____

   From exploring the discussion forums and other features of this site, what occupations and interests do you think the participants have?

   _____

   _____

   _____

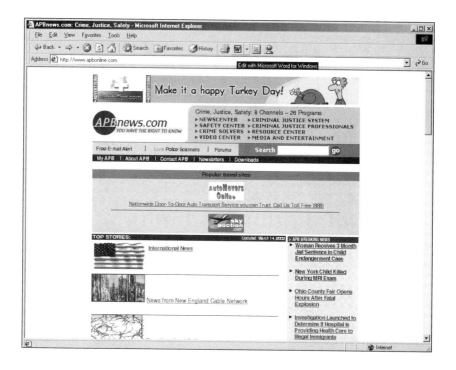

There are, of course, plenty of other Internet sources for crime news. Some people prefer sites like Cybersleuths.com (**http://www.cybersleuths. com**/) which are dedicated to unsolved cases. You should settle on your own favorite newspaper, magazine, or other source. There are two popular Mining Company guides on crime and justice, and the most active one is at **http://crime.about.com/**. Many people also rely upon the Drudge Report at **http://www.drudgereport.com** which allows you to scan the news wire services and read political commentary. Try to find a news source that is compatible with your interests and knowledge level.

Review Relevant Criminological Theories

New sites emerge all the time in this area, but the best sources currently are the comprehensive sites. Remember that these kinds of sites are typically put together by a faculty member for the benefit of their students and others around the Internet. There are several comprehensive sites in criminology and criminal justice to choose from.

1. Point your browser to **http://faculty.ncwc.edu/toconnor/ criminology.htm**
2. Scroll through the entire page without clicking on anything. Get a feel for the depth of content at a comprehensive site.

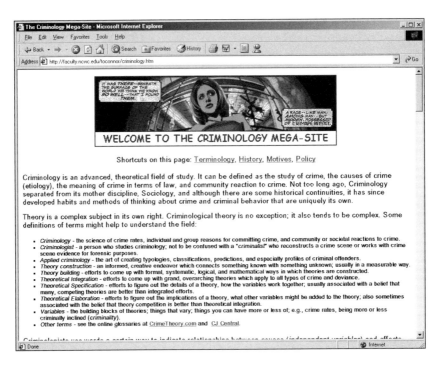

3. While thinking of a type of crime and the motives you suspect for it, read the two-column Table of Theory and Motives at this site.

Name one or two theories that match up with the motives you suspect are the cause of the crime you have in mind.

_____

_____

_____

Now look at the Table of Policy Implications at this site. Which ones match up with the theory or theories you had in mind?

_____

_____

_____

One of the features of this site is the History of Criminology page. Go to it, and then do a word search or Find (on this Page) with your browser to locate books with titles that match the ideas in your theory. What books did you find?

Other sites that are good comprehensive resources for criminological theory include the Redwood Highway (**http://www.sonoma.edu/cja/ info/infos.html**), and Cecil Greek's Criminal Justice Links (**http://www. criminology.fsu.edu/cj.html**). For strictly sociological theories, Socio-Realm at **http://www.digeratiweb.com/sociorealm** is your best bet, and for more biopsychological approaches, try CrimeTimes (**http://www. crime-times.org/**). You can also ask your instructor if he or she has a home page or a favorite site.

Check Out What the Think Tanks Think

There are numerous think tanks, research centers, institutes, and foundations in criminology and criminal justice. They have been extraordinarily influential in changing the shape of our justice system, as we know it. For example, our bail system would not be the same today if not for the Vera Institute (**http://www.vera.org/**), and we would not know as much as we do about detective work or the drug war without the Rand Corporation (**http://www.rand.org/**).

Some think tanks are affiliated with the government or a university, others are nonprofit organizations, and still others are philanthropic organizations. They invest lots of money into hiring the best talent and doing extensive research towards formulating policy papers on a wide range of issues. It is important you understand that think tanks are often supported by organizations with an ideological purpose; that is, they are usually progressive or conservative. You will find an inordinate number of them devoted to victim's rights, women's rights, children's rights, and drunk driving simply because these are areas which draw the most activism.

1. Point your browser to **http://www.policy.com/**
2. Take a moment to look over the opening page and see if there are any crime and justice issues highlighted by a special banner or button, but don't click on them right now.
3. Somewhere in the left margin there should be a lengthy table of contents. Scroll down until you see the words "Think Tanks," which may be under the heading of "Community." Click on "Think Tanks." You should see an alphabetical list of hundreds of think tanks.

iSearch: Criminal Justice

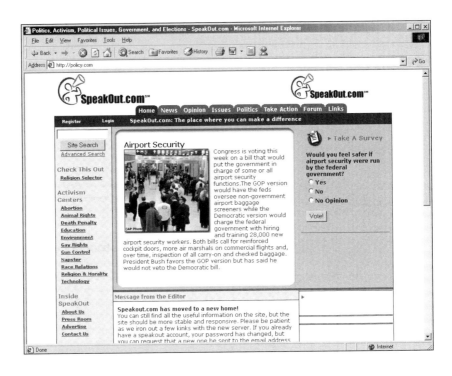

Read the descriptions of the various think tanks (or perhaps do a word search or Find (on this Page) with your browser for words like "crime" and "justice"). Which think tanks are most directly relevant to criminology and criminal justice?

_____

_____

_____

Which think tanks are not directly relevant, but secondarily relevant, or connected with the root causes of crime or problems in criminal justice?

_____

_____

_____

For at least two of the think tanks, click on their links and view their home pages. Would you label them as progressive or conservative? Name the think tank and its ideological perspective.

_____

_____

_____

Most people can only keep track of a handful of think tanks. As you can see from their Web pages, these sites include an extensive amount of information. So, there's a real need for an indexing service like policy.com. Another site that many people find helpful is the Electronic Policy Network at **http://www.epn.org**—though it is more health and welfare oriented while policy.com is more crime and justice oriented. This should not matter much, however, since you're looking for reports on what is behind the crime problem, like broken homes or lack of employment opportunities.

Also, as you've discovered, it's difficult to tell which think tanks really have a direct relevance to criminology and criminal justice. You might find the site called Interest Groups in Criminal Justice (**http://faculty.ncwc. edu/toconnor/thnktank.htm**) helpful in this regard, as it lists the most relevant ones for you. Other good sites to search for expert opinion include the AAAS Directory of Human Rights Resources (**http://shr.aaas.org/ dhr.htm**), the IGC JusticeNet (**http://www.igc.org**), John Fuller's Peacemaking and Crime (**http://www.westga.edu/~jfuller/peace.html**), and Critical Criminology's Home Page (**http://www.critcrim.org/**), although the latter two might require a bit of exploring.

Agree or Disagree with the ACLU

Welcome to the most powerful lobby group in criminology and criminal justice, followed only by the ABA (**http://www.abanet.org/**) and perhaps the NRA (**http://www.nra.org/**). The purpose of this exercise is to explore some of the resources on the ACLU home page and to develop your critical judgment skills.

The American Civil Liberties Union was founded in 1920, about the same time as the NAACP, and the two organizations have always worked closely together, despite serious disagreements on matters such as the ACLU's support of free speech rights for people espousing doctrines of white supremacy. It's not that the ACLU supports white supremacy. It's just that the ACLU will fight extremely hard to protect everyone's constitutional rights to the fullest, including flag burning and other controversial actions.

1. Point your browser to **http://www.aclu.org/**
2. Take a moment to look over any highlights of current events on the opening page and locate the table of contents, which should be in the right margin.

On the opening page, what featured top stories are marked high priority, immediate alert, or otherwise suggesting the viewer take action? Do you think this is an effective attention-grabbing device? Did it make

iSearch: Criminal Justice

you feel empowered, or at least curious, that you could take action on something?

_____

_____

_____

In the table of contents, click on the words "criminal justice." Then, click on the main highlighted story on that page, and read the short essay. What is the ACLU's position? Do you support what they are recommending or do you think they are making too much out of it?

_____

_____

_____

Now, go back to the home page table of contents and click on the word "prisons." Read the short essay called Prisoners' Rights in a Free

Society. Do you agree or disagree that more and more prisons are becoming unfit for human habitation?

_____

_____

_____

The ACLU is not the only place, of course, where you can exercise critical judgment or learn about individual rights. You might want to check out the UN High Commission on Human Rights (**http://www.unhchr.ch/**), constitutional rights in other countries (**http://www.uni-wuerzburg.de/ law/index.html**), or Amnesty International (**http://www.amnesty.org/**). It's often the case that a comparative perspective provides a fresh way of looking at things. Many people regard the Amnesty International's statement against the death penalty as the most persuasive argument against it.

Evaluate Professional Associations and Their Journals

Let's assume the time has come in your professional career to join an association of your peers. You know that doing so reflects credibility, expertise, and some prestige upon yourself. You will have the chance to attend conferences, present papers, win awards, gain recognition, and have an outlet for your publications. This publication outlet would usually be a journal subscription that comes free with your membership subscription. Having a journal subscription also allows you to keep up with the latest developments in your field. By the way, student memberships are usually available at a significantly reduced rate.

The question then becomes: which associations should you join? Most people have limited budgets and can't join them all. What you need is a Web site that lists the various associations and the journals they provide. As of this printing, nothing like that which fits the bill perfectly exists on the Internet, but a Web site that does list quite a few associations is Frank Schmallenger's Cybrary.

1. Point your browser to **http://www.cjcentral.com/**
2. Click on the item marked "Dr. Frank Schmallenger's Criminal Justice Cybrary" and once this page loads, click on "Show All Categories".
3. Once the lengthy list of categories is seen, look for and click on the phrase "Associations in Criminal Justice". A lengthy list of professional associations should appear in your browser.

Notice the names of the different associations. Some of them are called Boards and others are called Societies. Click on one or two examples of each. From reading their mission statements, does it seem like there's a difference between a board and other types of associations?

_____

_____

_____

Find and click on the link for the American Board of Criminalistics. Explore everything on this site by clicking on anything provided: Overview, Examinations, Roster, Newsletter, and Information. What are the typical occupations of people who join this association? Does membership come with a journal subscription?

_____

_____

_____

Now, find and click on the American Society of Criminology. Read the online membership form. Are student rates available? Does membership come with a journal subscription?

_____

_____

_____

Since this exercise also involves evaluating online journals, go back to the main listing of associations, and click on different associations until you find one with an online newsletter or journal. Click on their newsletter or journal and read it. Do you find it directly relevant to criminology and criminal justice?

_____

_____

_____

This exercise makes the process of selecting a professional association more scientific than it has to be. Most people, in real life, join different groups on the basis of hit-and-miss or word-of-mouth. There is general agreement that the American Society of Criminology (**http://www.asc41. com/**) and the Academy of Criminal Justice Sciences (**http://www.acjs. org/**) are the top associations with the best journals at reduced student membership rates.

For your particular career interests, however, you may want to join a more specialized association—one dedicated to policing or private security, for example. To find out about these, you can visit any police mega-site. A good starting place is The Best of CJ: Professional Organizations (**http://faculty.ncwc.edu/toconnor/linklist.htm#PROF**).

If you need help in determining the differences between a journal, a newsletter, a magazine, and a 'Zine, then check out Cornell University's Research Skills (**http://www.library.cornell.edu/okuref/research/skill20.html**) which distinguishes scholarly and non-scholarly periodicals.

Get Government Grant Money

Let's assume you've finally graduated from college and you're working at a famous research think tank or you've landed an entry-level managerial position in a justice or social service agency. Part of your job description may require that you write grants to receive government funding. More and more job descriptions are requiring the ability to obtain grants. The Internet is the best place to start developing that ability. In the field of criminology and criminal justice, there is no better place to begin the search for government grant money than the Justice Information Center, maintained by NCJRS, or the National Criminal Justice Reference Service.

1. Point your browser to **http://www.ncjrs.org/**

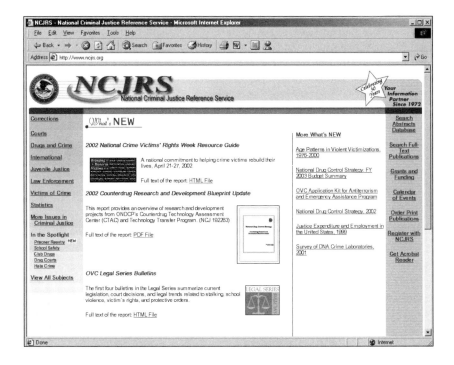

iSearch: Criminal Justice

2. Ignore the fancy image map that shows up on the top of the page. Scroll down the page until you find and click on the button or words **Justice Grants.**

How many individual Justice Department agencies provide funds to researchers? Are there any other agencies suggested on this page as possible places to look for federal grants? If so, what are they? Are there any grant announcements or solicitations that have been cancelled?

Click on each of these individual agencies to see how the new address or URL changes in your browser. Which agencies take you to a completely different URL? What agencies offering grants provide the most information via their Web site?

Look over the various grant opportunities at the individual agencies, either by reading the descriptions on the Justice Grants page or by exploring specific grant links themselves. From looking over the grant opportunities, are there any you could apply for where the deadline has not been reached?

As this exercise made apparent, sometimes there are government agencies other than the Justice Department involved in grant opportunities for criminology and criminal justice. To look at the Web sites for these other agencies, you need a site like the Federal Web Locator (**http://www. infoctr.edu/fwl/**) or a site containing links to federal agencies. Experienced researchers also have learned how to use the search engine for the Federal Register. This was presented to you on the Justice Grants page (**http://www.ncjrs.org/fedgrant.html**).

Finding the appropriate government grant is a little like searching the Internet for financial aid. At least, that's the idea behind a site called the Community of Science (**http://www.cos.com/**) where you can find a section for undergraduate student research grants in the form of fellowships and scholarships.

State governments also have grant programs. Simply locate the home page for your state government and check their index, site map, or appropriate agency pages for grant opportunities. In addition, even though this exercise was focused on getting government grant money, you should not neglect looking into philanthropic organizations or private foundations. The Foundation Center (**http://fdncenter.org/**) is the gateway for private grants.

Take a Stand on a Crime Bill

Each year, hundreds of bills are introduced on the floor of the U.S. House or Senate. In this exercise, we will look at how you can easily locate a bill that relates to crime, any of your particular interests, or any proposed legislation that might affect the operations of the agency you work for. Whether or not you want to express a personal activism, it helps in almost all employment situations to stay on top of proposed legislation that might affect your area of work. You should also not hesitate to email your representative in Congress to take a stand. To do this, you need timely information on exactly how far a bill has progressed. If it has passed both houses of Congress, you may have to email the President.

1. Point your browser to **http://thomas.loc.gov/.**

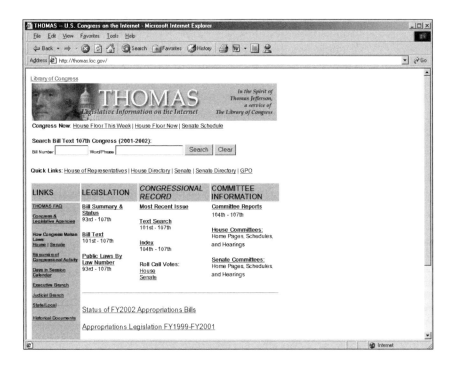

2. Look for the input box that is Search Current Congress for Text of Bills, by Word/Phrase. Leave the box that says by Bill Number blank. Type the word "crime" in the by Word/Phrase box, and hit the search button.

How many crime bills have been proposed in the current Congress, according to the results of your search? Look over this list of crime bills Exclude those that are not really crime bills, but changes in the tax code, creation of new holidays, etc. How many crime bills are there now?

_____

_____

_____

Go ahead and click on at least three crime bills that might interest you. The link to read the bill is usually located after its name in the form of a number, like S521 or HR2061. What are these crime bills about?

_____

_____

_____

For one of the bills that interest you, find out who introduced the bill, and what the disposition is. Who introduced the bill? What happened to the bill? Was it sent to committee, passed in one house but not the other, or passed and sent on to the President? Would you feel comfortable emailing a letter of support or opposition to the appropriate elected official?

_____

_____

_____

Look for a Better Job

Both salaries and cost of living vary widely in criminology and criminal justice, depending upon where you live in the country. A salary of $25,000 might get you by in some parts of the South, but it certainly won't pay the rent in New York City. What you need is an Internet guide to average salaries and cost of living. One particularly useful Web site is the Occupational Outlook Handbook (**http://www.umsl.edu/services/govdocs/ooh20002001/1.htm**), which gives you information on salaries, work descriptions, qualifications, and growth trends; that is, whether your job is a dead-end or at least expected to grow moderately. This handbook is put together by economists, and some colleges even use it to plan which

iSearch: Criminal Justice

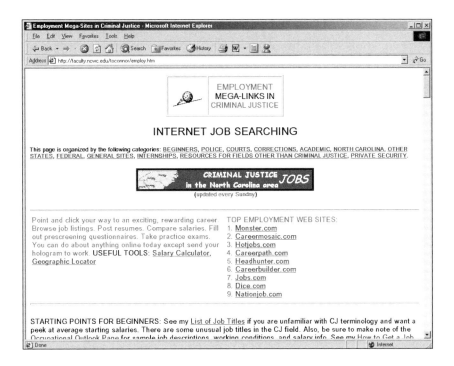

majors to offer. Another popular Web site is the Salary/Moving Calculators from HomeFair (**http://www2.homefair.com/calc/salcalc.html**). At this site, you plug in the name of the town you're thinking about moving to and your current address. You'll find out how much more or less you need to earn in order to afford your move. HomeFair can also calculate crime rate differences.

There are plenty of Internet employment guides in criminology and criminal justice. A few of them charge a subscription fee and others will constantly try to sell you booklets, but, by and large, the people who put together these guides have been pretty generous. This exercise will involve looking at one of these sites. It's free, regularly updated, and called Employment MegaLinks in Criminal Justice.

1. Point your browser to **http://faculty.ncwc.edu/toconnor/employ. htm.**

   Judging from the number of links available, what area of work (policing, courts, corrections, other) seems to be emphasized at this site? What area of work is neglected?

   _____

   _____

   _____

What does the phrase "open recruitment" mean? Indicate to what levels of government (local, county, state, or federal) this phrase applies.

_____

_____

_____

Good vocational guidance while you're still in college can be found at Dr. Carlie's AdviseNet (**http://courses.smsu.edu/mkc096f/**). For aspiring graduate students and professionals, the Email Mentoring Program of the American Society of Criminology (**http://sun.soci.niu.edu/~ascmentr/ mentor.html**) matches your interests with an academic or practitioner who can give you sound professional advice.

Any of the megasites in criminology and criminal justice should have an employment advice or links page. One site that includes a unique collection of police links is Ira Wilsker's Law Enforcement Sites on the Web (**http://www.ih2000.net/ira/ira2.htm#jobs**).

iSearch: Criminal Justice

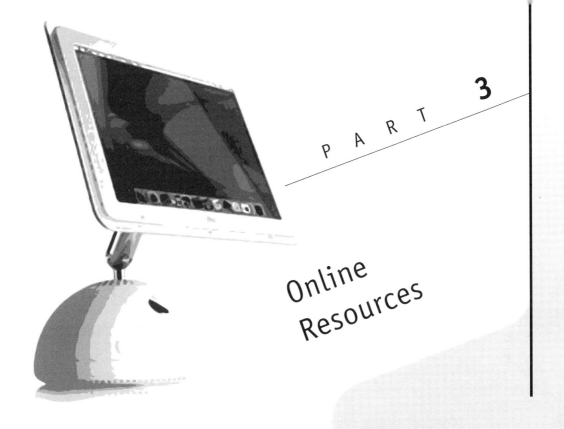

Online
Resources

Internet Sites Useful in Criminology and Criminal Justice

Criminology and Criminal Justice Mega-sites

Allyn and Bacon's Criminal Justice Links

http://www.abacon.com/sociology/soclinks/cj.html

An extensive collection of links to sites in victimology, policing, the courts and law, forensics, corrections, the death penalty, associations, and government and international organizations.

Charles Dreveskracht's Web site

http://arapaho.nsuok.edu/~dreveskr/

A site created by Professor Charles Dreveskracht at Northeastern State University with numerous links on topics in comparative criminology, victimology, criminal justice history, criminal justice research, and Native American resources. The site also includes criminal justice education and career resources, as well as numerous links to information about September 11, 2001 and its aftermath.

Crime Connections on the Web

`http://www.justiceblind.com/links.html`

A site created by Professor Matt Robinson at Appalachian State University with numerous links on topics in criminology, criminal justice, and government. The site also includes criminal justice education and drug links. This new location is organized around his book's format.

Crime Theory.com

`http://www.crimetheory.com/`

A site created by Professor Bruce Hoffman at the University of Washington with numerous links and original documents on the history, timeline, and major figures of criminology, including research topics, learning resources, and classroom assignments. The site is for both instructors and students, and also features a link of the month.

Criminal Justice Education Web

`http://www.cjed.com/`

A site created by Professor Philip Reichel at the University of Northern Colorado with numerous links on careers, research topics, writing, teaching, and classroom assignments. The site is for both instructors and students, and also contains correctional and international resources.

Criminal Justice Links

`http://www.criminology.fsu.edu/cj.html`

A site created by Professor Cecil Greek at Florida State University with numerous links arranged under topics in crime prevention, delinquency, drugs, law, obscenity, forensics, policing, the courts, corrections, international links, criminal justice education, crime in the media, criminal justice images and illustrations, and online criminal justice discussion groups and E-journals. The site also contains sample book chapters and a navigable map of the criminal justice system.

Criminal Justice MegaLinks

`http://faculty.ncwc.edu/toconnor`

A site created by Professor Tom O'Connor at North Carolina Wesleyan College with numerous links arranged by areas of interest in criminology, law,

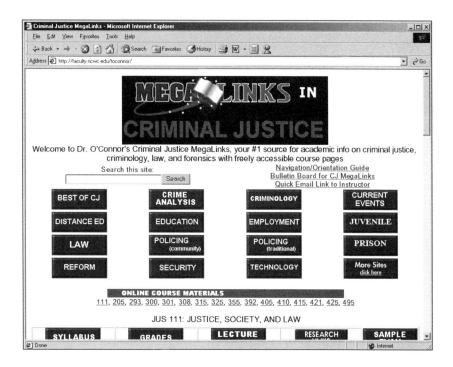

crime analysis, current events, juvenile justice, policing, prisons, system re-form, computer security, criminal justice education, distance education, criminal justice technology, and criminal justice employment. The site also contains online lectures, sample exams, and a listing of the Best Sites in criminal justice.

Cybrary of Criminal Justice

`http://talkjustice.com/cybrary.asp`

A site created by Dr. Frank Schmalleger at the Justice Research Association with numerous links arranged in a Top 100 format and by categories and subcategories in criminal justice, criminology, law, criminal justice careers, criminal justice technology, discussion lists, journals, and 'Zines. The site also contains a glossary of criminal justice terms and a chat room.

JusticeLink (U.K.)

`http://www.kcl.ac.uk/depsta/rel/ccjs/justicelink/`
`general.htm`

A site created by Dr. Simon Marshall at the U.K. Centre for Crime and Jus-tice Studies that contains many U.K. and U.S. links on criminology, law,

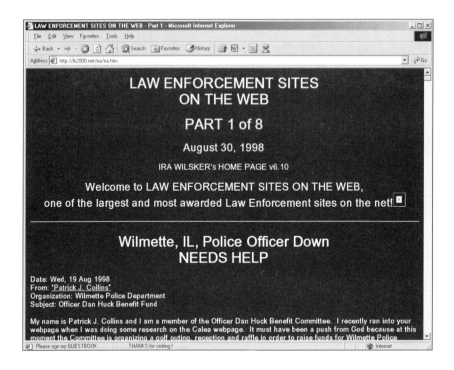

policing, probation, prisons, criminology journals, international organizations, and international issues in criminal justice.

Law Enforcement Sites on the Web

`http://www.ih2000.net/ira/ira.htm`

A site created by Professor Ira Wilsker at Lamar University arranged by large pages of links on police departments, employment, domestic violence, forensics, drugs, corrections, law, the courts, and corrections. The site also contains terrorism links, computer crime links, and miscellaneous links.

Links to Criminal Justice Related Sites

`http://cjwww.csustan.edu/cj/links.html`

A site created by Professor Phyllis Gerstenfeld at California State University-Stanislaw with many links categorized by civil liberties, hate crimes, law enforcement, corrections, forensics, juvenile justice, law, social science, and politics.

iSearch: Criminal Justice

Redwood Highway

http://www.sonoma.edu/cja/info/infos.html

A site created by Professor Pat Jackson at Sonoma State University with numerous links arranged by pages on criminology, law enforcement, law and the courts, corrections, special issues like the death penalty, system reform, international links, and electronic journals.

Web of Justice

http://www.co.pinellas.fl.us/bcc/juscoord/explore.htm

A site created by Tim Burns, an information analyst at the Pinellas County (FL) department of Justice Coordination with many links arranged by areas of interest in corrections, probation and parole, the courts, law enforcement, government, and international criminal justice.

Academic Sites

University of Alaska at Anchorage

http://www.uaa.alaska.edu/just/

The Justice Center at this school has an extremely comprehensive collection of links and online articles on issues of the death penalty, racism, human rights, victims, law enforcement, law, juvenile justice, the courts, and corrections.

Arizona State University

http://www.asu.edu/copp/justice/

ASU's School of Justice Studies has extensive Internet resources on women's studies, Latino studies, alternative dispute resolution, mediation, fairness in media, and reform of drug laws.

University of Arkansas at Little Rock

http://www.ualr.edu/~cjdept/

This Department of Criminal Justice Web site has a list of honor societies in criminal justice, information about distance education, and links on corrections, human rights topics, law, policing, and computer technology.

California Lutheran University

http://robles.callutheran.edu/scj/scj.html

This Department of Criminal Justice has an extremely useful Web site with links categorized by corrections, gangs, criminal investigation, crime

iSearch: Criminal Justice

prevention, the courts, juvenile delinquency, law enforcement, law, sentencing, and substance abuse.

University of Delaware

http://www.udel.edu/soc/homepage.htm

This Department of Sociology and Criminal Justice houses the Disaster Research Center and a Center for Drug and Alcohol Studies.

Eastern Kentucky University

http://www.len.eku.edu/

This College of Justice and Safety Web site has links and online publications about community policing and public safety.

Florida Gulf Coast University

http://spss.fgcu.edu/cj/

This Division of Criminal Justice Web site contains links on associations, government, the courts, corrections, and juvenile justice.

Florida State University

http://www.criminology.fsu.edu/

FSU's School of Criminology and Criminal Justice has distance education information, affiliated associations, publications, links to various Police Corps nationwide, and the Criminal Justice Links site.

University of Illinois at Chicago

http://www.uic.edu/depts/cjus/

The UIC Department of Criminal Justice Web site has two notable institutes and centers on it. The Institute for Public Safety Partnership has extensive resources on community policing with multimedia clips. The Office of International Criminal Justice has online journals and archived documents.

Illinois State University

http://www.ilstu.edu/depts/cjs/

This Department of Criminal Justice Web site has resource pages on criminal justice history, rural crime, and drugs.

Indiana University of Pennsylvania

http://www.chss.iup.edu/cr

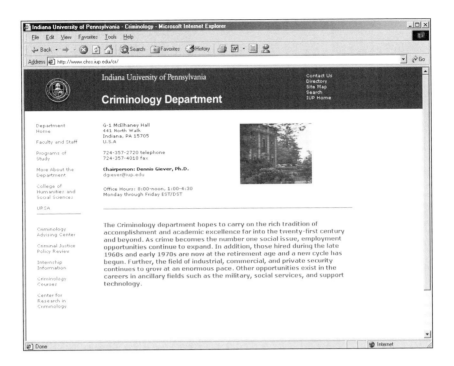

IUP's Department of Criminology has a research-oriented collection of links and online abstracts from the journal, Criminal Justice Policy Review.

John Jay College of Criminal Justice

`http://www.jjay.cuny.edu/index.html`

This college serves as a major research center for education and research in criminal justice, law enforcement, and forensic science.

University of Maryland

`http://www.bsos.umd.edu/ccjs/`

This college's Web site has information on technology, substance abuse, recidivism, and other research activities.

University of Memphis

`http://cjustice.memphis.edu`

This department's Web site has a rather unique resource directory on the topic of genocide, an interest of most of the faculty members.

Michigan State University

http://www.dj.msu.edu

MSU's School of Criminal Justice has online career information, distance education programs, and useful faculty member home pages.

University of Nebraska at Omaha

http://www.unomaha.edu/~crimjust/

This Department of Criminal Justice Web site has a list of links and houses a center for the study of community policing which has some information.

Northern Arizona University

http://www.nau.edu/~crimj-p/

This Department of Criminal Justice Web site has some good faculty member home pages and a prelaw page that helps you decide if going to law school is the right idea.

Pennsylvania State University

http://www.la.psu.edu/admj/welcome.htm

PSU's Program in Crime, Law, and Justice has a Web site that contains a link under Other Sites of Interest to their school's library page which is a megasite for the topics of delinquency, victimization, and sentencing.

Portland State University

http://www.upa.pdx.edu/AJ/

This Division of Administration of Justice has an extensive set of criminal justice links on the topics of law enforcement, law, news, and guns.

Rutgers, the State University of New Jersey

http://rutgers-newark.rutgers.edu/rscj/

This School of Criminal Justice Web site has a good collection of links on corrections and the courts. It also houses a Center for Crime Prevention, the World Criminal Justice Library Network, and the NCCD (National Council on Crime and Delinquency) collection of monographs and dissertations.

Sam Houston State University

http://www.shsu.edu/cjcenter/

This site is really three sites in one. There's the College of Criminal Justice, a Law Enforcement Institute, and a Corrections Institute. Each one has extensive criminal justice links and some online publications.

San Jose State University

http://www.sjsu.edu/depts/casa/aj/index.html

This Department of Administration of Justice has a small, but good, collection of links on human rights, corrections, law enforcement, forensics, and juvenile justice. Click on the tab for "Resources" to get to the links.

University of South Carolina

http://www.sc.edu/crju/

This college has a small, but good collection of links on law enforcement, corrections, courts, victimology, and firearms.

iSearch: Criminal Justice

Southern Illinois University

http://www.siu.edu/~ajsiuc/

This Department of Administration of Justice has a Web page on crime mapping and how to read a map.

Southwest Texas State University

http://www.cj.swt.edu/

This department's Web site has a well-organized collection of Internet resources on policing, courts, corrections, probation, and parole.

State University of New York at Albany

http://www.albany.edu/scj/

SUNY-Albany's School of Criminal Justice Web site has some career information, faculty home pages, and extensive links on law, the courts, corrections, the death penalty, drugs, and victims. It also houses the Sourcebook of Criminal Justice Statistics and the Journal of Criminal Justice and Popular Culture.

Temple University

http://www.temple.edu/cjus/

This Department of Criminal Justice Web site has a couple of excellent faculty member home pages with resources on white-collar crime, hate crime, sentencing, race and crime, and drugs.

University of Southern Mississippi

http://www.cj.usm.edu/

This Department of Criminal Justice Web site has a collection of links on family and juvenile studies, policing, corrections, law, and a link to Adam McKee's criminal justice page, which is a separate resource in itself.

Government Resources

Alcohol, Tobacco and Firearms

http://www.atf.treas.gov/

A Treasury Department bureau charged with reducing crime, collecting revenue, and protecting the public. It also investigates explosions, bombings, and arsons.

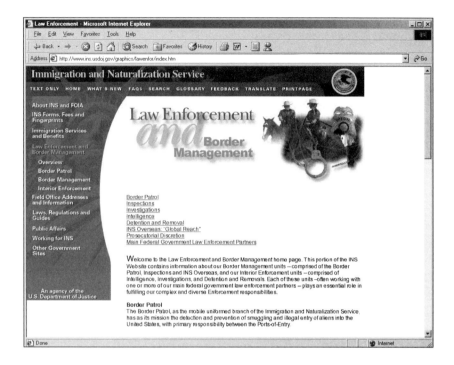

Border Patrol

http://www.ins.usdoj.gov/graphics/lawenfor/index.htm

A branch of the Justice Department's Immigration and Naturalization Service charged with enforcement of the immigration laws.

Bureau of Prisons

http://www.bop.gov/

The U.S. Bureau of Prisons manages a hundred federal prisons at all levels of security. Their Web site offers information on their prisoners, employment information, and other facts.

Customs

http://www.customs.ustreas.gov/

The U.S. Customs Service is charged with ensuring lawful trade and travel.

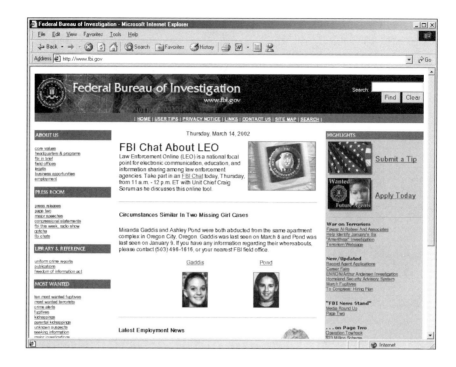

Drug Enforcement Administration

http://www.usdoj.gov/dea/

A Justice Department agency charged with enforcement of all controlled substances in the United States.

Federal Bureau of Investigation

http://www.fbi.gov/

A Justice Department agency with a broad mandate to investigate all other crimes not assigned to any other federal agency.

Federal Judicial Center

http://www.fjc.gov/

This site is the home page of the research and continuing education wing for the federal courts, and the site consists of downloadable publications covering a wide range of topics, from sentencing guidelines to information about habeas corpus writs.

Federal Judiciary Home Page

http://www.uscourts.gov/

This is a site set up for the general public to assist in understanding of how court systems operate. Their publication, "About the U.S. Courts," is excellent, and the site covers both state and federal court systems.

FedWorld

http://www.fedworld.gov

A site that offers quick access to thousands of United States government Web sites, online government documents, databases, and other information.

House of Representatives

http://www.house.gov

A quick and easy way to locate and contact your representative.

Library of Congress

http://lcweb.loc.gov

Online resources that are considered useful to the American people and to sustain and preserve a universal collection of knowledge for future generations. Contains topical and historical collections as well as other featured exhibitions.

National Archive of Criminal Justice Data

http://www.icpsr.umich.edu/NACJD/

Large, downloadable datasets that have been deposited by government-funded researchers in hopes that someone else can "mine" the data through secondary analysis and extract more conclusions than the original researchers did.

National Clearinghouse on Child Abuse and Neglect

http://www.calib.com/nccanch/

Funded by the Children's Bureau, this organization acts as an information resource for people seeking information on prevention, identification, and treatment of child abuse and neglect.

National Consortium for Justice Information and Statistics

http://www.search.org/

Funded by the government, this organization conducts symposiums and conferences designed to improve the information gathering and dissemination functions of justice agencies. It acts as a clearinghouse of information on the latest software solutions, maintains a shareware library, and produces some publications.

National Crime Victimization Survey (NCVS)

http://www.ojp.usdoj.gov/bjs/cvict.htm

This site is one of the major sources of crime data in the form of victim surveys. The survey results are usually portrayed as the number of households touched by crime.

National Criminal Justice Reference Service

http://www.ncjrs.org/

The most extensive resource of information of criminal and juvenile justice in the world. NCJRS is a collection of clearinghouses supporting all bureaus of the Department of Justice, Office of Justice Programs, the National Institute of Justice, the Office of Juvenile Justice and Delinquency Prevention, the Bureau of Justice Statistics, the Bureau of Justice Assistance, and the Office for Victims of Crime. It also supports the Office of National Drug Control Policy.

National Incident-Based Reporting System (NIBRS)

http://www.nibrs.search.org/

This is a home page of the NIBRS project which will eventually replace the Uniform Crime Report (UCR) format that the FBI presently uses.

National Institute of Corrections

http://www.nicic.org/inst/

Funded by the Justice Department and technically part of the Bureau of Prisons, the NIC provides training programs in corrections and carries out objective research on corrections. Their Web site offers a collection of prison-related Internet resources as well as access to some of their own publications.

National Law Enforcement and Corrections Technology Center

http://www.nlectc.org/

An exhaustive resource of information on currently used and soon-to-be-developed crime-fighting technology. The site maintains a database of less-than-lethal weaponry, protective equipment, and surveillance devices in

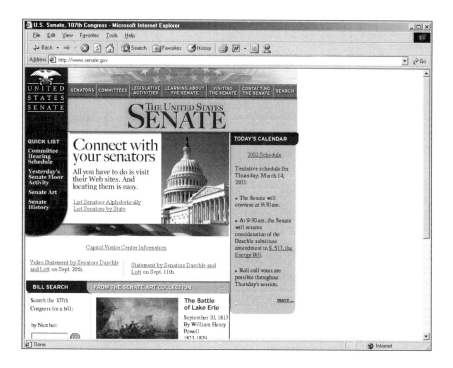

various stages of commercialization and development. It also provides up-dates on the forensic uses of DNA and crime mapping technology.

Senate Home Page

http://www.senate.gov/

A quick and easy way to locate and contact your senator.

Sourcebook of Criminal Justice Statistics

http://www.albany.edu/sourcebook/

Funded by the Justice Department, the Sourcebook contains over 600 of the most important tables of numbers on characteristics of the criminal jus-tice system, characteristics of criminal offenders, and public opinion about crime and the criminal justice system.

Thomas—U.S. Congress on the Internet

http://thomas.loc.gov/

Access to the latest crime bills, laws, Congressional Record, reports, and links to further information.

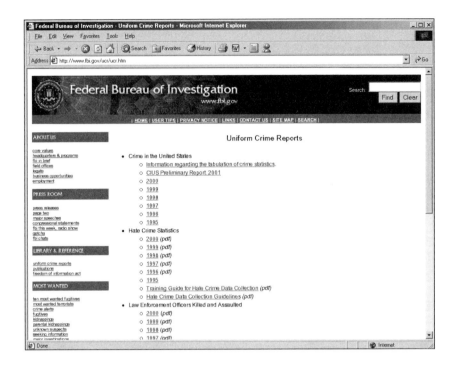

Uniform Crime Reports (UCR)

http://www.fbi.gov/ucr.htm

The official crime rates for the United States, available for viewing.

United Nations Crime and Justice Information Network

http://www.uncjin.org

Extensive information on international crimes like money laundering, bribery, and corruption.

U.S. Attorney's Manual

http://www.usdoj.gov/usao/eousa/foia_reading_room/usam/

This site details exactly what a United States attorney is supposed to do, how to act, and how to function. The site also explains the role of a prosecutor.

iSearch: Criminal Justice

U.S. Department of Justice

http://www.usdoj.gov/

Cabinet-level agency consisting of many branches, including the FBI and DEA, who are charged with enforcement of all federal crimes.

U.S. Intelligence Community

http://www.odci.gov/ic/

A group of about thirteen agencies, including the CIA, who are charged with defending the national security.

U.S. Marshals

http://www.usdoj.gov/marshals/

A Service within the Justice Department that is responsible for protecting the judiciary, federal witnesses, transporting federal prisoners, and managing seized assets.

U.S. Parole Commission

http://www.usdoj.gov/uspc/

A bureau within the Justice Department that sets policy and conditions affecting federal parolees and the work of federal probation and parole officers. Their site has a rather lengthy document explaining how the parole system works.

U.S. Postal Inspectors

http://www.usps.gov/websites/depart/inspect/

A federal agency charged with enforcing a variety of crimes, like blackmail, mail fraud, child pornography, and counterfeiting.

U.S. Sentencing Commission

http://www.ussc.gov/

An informative site with many guidelines on various aspects of sentencing, including trends, issues, and the ongoing movement towards guidelines.

iSearch: Criminal Justice

White House Social Statistics Briefing Room

http://www.whitehouse.gov/fsbr/crime.html

This site is what the President's office uses to keep track of various crime summaries.

Professional Associations

Academy of Criminal Justice Sciences

http://www.acjs.org/

The ACJS is one of the premier associations for criminal justice educators and professionals. The site maintains links to its regional associations, and provides a set of links to various Internet resources such as criminal justice related newsletters, mailing lists, and Web pages of its members.

American Academy of Forensic Sciences

http://www.aafs.org/

The AAFS consists of scientists, lawyers, physicians, criminalists, toxicologists, dentists, physical anthropologists, document examiners, engineers, psychiatrists, and educators with an interest in forensic science. Their Web site contains career information and links of interest.

American Bar Association

http://www.abanet.org/

An association for lawyers and law students, the ABA Web site has extensive online resources for the general public on law, domestic violence, homelessness, drugs, and juvenile justice.

American Board of Criminalistics

http://www.criminalistics.com/

The ABC is an organization of forensic scientists that are involved in work requiring board certification. This site has a list of graduate programs in forensic science.

American Judicature Society

http://www.ajs.org/

This is an association of judges. Their Web site has extensive resources on judicial selection, judicial conduct, judicial independence, and other issues of importance to judges.

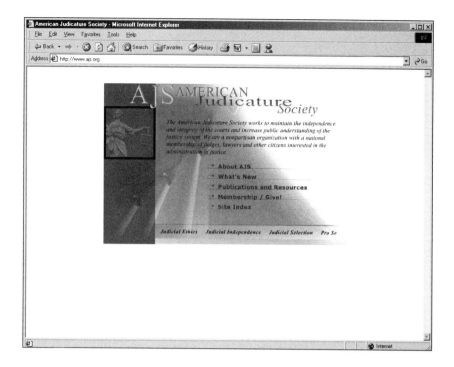

American Psychiatric Association

http://www.psych.org/

A medical specialty society with over 40,000 members specialized in the diagnosis and treatment of mental and emotional illness and substance use disorders.

American Society of Criminology

http://www.asc41.com/

The ASC is one of the premier associations for criminology and criminal justice educators and professionals. The site maintains links to its divisions, employment listings, and other sites of interest to criminologists.

American Society for Industrial Security

http://www.asisonline.org/

ASIS is the premier association for private security professionals. Their extensive Web site provides information about careers, news of interest to security and protection professionals, and other items.

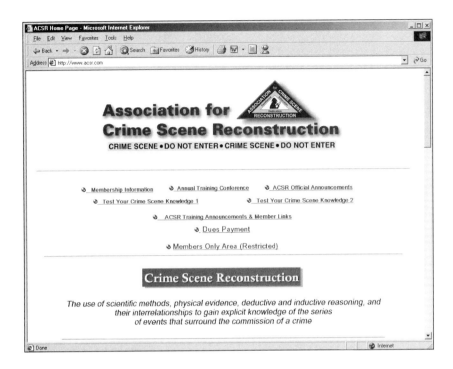

Association for Crime Scene Reconstruction

http://www.acsr.com/

ACSR is a group of investigators, forensic experts, and teachers who work on the development and study of deductive and inductive reasoning skills in drawing inferences from crime scene evidence. Their site contains a Test Your Crime Scene Knowledge quiz.

British Society of Criminology

http://www.lboro.ac.uk/departments/ss/BSC/homepage/
HOMEPAGE.HTM

This association's Web site has information about the society, workshops, seminars, ways to stay in touch with its six branches, links of interest, and a Web journal.

High Technology Crime Investigation Association

http://htcia.org

HTCIA is a group of investigators who study the special techniques necessary for dealing with crimes involving technology more advanced than traditional techniques or departments can handle.

International Association of Chiefs of Police

http://www.theiacp.org/

This premier law enforcement association Web site has quite a bit of information arranged alphabetically by topic. Sample topics include the police response to domestic violence and their legislative agenda.

International Association of Correctional Officers

http://www.oicj.org/public/

This site is home to "The Keeper's Voice," an online newsletter, and contains information, news, and articles on prison life, prison programs, and prisoner rights.

International Association of Directors of Law Enforcement Standards and Training

http://www.iadlest.org/

IADLEST is an association of training managers involved in the training of law enforcement officers. Their site contains a state member directory which is a list of links to every police officer certification authority nationwide.

International Association for Identification

http://www.theiai.org

This is a law enforcement association consisting mostly of crime scene investigators and crime lab workers. Their Web site has extensive resources on various forensic techniques, such as fingerprinting and forensic art, as well as numerous other links to resources on the Internet or on their site.

International Association of Law Enforcement Planners

http://www.ialep.org/

IALEP is an association of police executive staff who network and share common interests. Their Web site contains reports from their meetings, other important announcements, and links of interest to their members.

International Association of Women Police

http://www.iawp.org/

This association Web site has tons of information, including related links, on the policewomen's movement and an online magazine.

iSearch: Criminal Justice

International Community Corrections Association

http://www.iccaweb.org/

The site contains information about the history of halfway houses and how the community corrections movement has grown today.

National Criminal Justice Association

http://www.sso.org/ncja/

A group in Washington, D.C. that represents state and local governments to lobby for more effective crime control legislation. They produce a series of monthly and quarterly publications, some of which can be viewed from their Web site.

National Drug Enforcement Officers Association

http://www.ndeoa.org/

NDEOA is a group of law enforcement officers who work or have an interest in drug enforcement. Their Web site contains information about meeting announcements and links of interest.

National Legal Aid and Defender Association

http://www.nlada.org/d-perform.htm

This site contains a set of performance standards that defense lawyers are judged by. There is also information on the general duties and functions of defense lawyers.

National Organization of Black Law Enforcement Executives

http://www.noblenatl.org/

NOBLE is the premier law enforcement organization for African Americans. Their site is news-oriented and contains information on scholarship and grant opportunities.

National Association of Blacks in Criminal Justice

http://www.nabcj.org/

NABCJ is an association of African Americans working in the criminal justice system; as police, in the courts, or in corrections. Their Web site has a newsletter, meeting announcements, and links of interest.

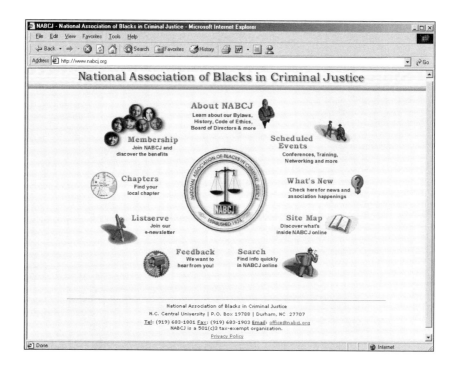

National Sheriffs Association

`http://www.sheriffs.org/`

A group dedicated to furthering professionalism and sharing ideas in criminal justice.

Police Executive Research Forum

`http://www.policeforum.org/`

PERF is one of the premier associations in criminal justice, based on the idea that academics and police executives can work together to devise innovative, creative changes. Their Web site contains sample publications, downloadable databases, and a collection of Internet resources.

Society for Police and Criminal Psychology

`http://cep.jmu.edu/spcp`

SPCP is an association of academics and professionals with an interest in all aspects of psychology applied to the criminal justice system. Their Web site contains information about their meetings, a diplomate program, and a list of forensic psychology graduate programs.

iSearch: Criminal Justice

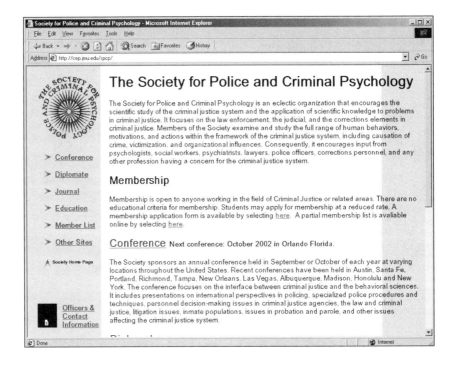

Society of Police Futurists International

http://www.policefuturists.org/

This association consists of academics and professionals who have an interest in futurism and futurist studies, and how those long-range forecasts have implications for practical criminal justice work. Their Web site consists of issue papers, links of interest, and membership information.

Specialty Areas

COMPUTER CRIME

Center for Democracy and Technology

http://www.cdt.org/

A news-oriented site that focuses upon encryption and other government initiatives related to ensuring a future of safer computing.

Computer Crime Research Resources

http://mailer.fsu.edu/~btf1553/ccrr/welcome.htm

An incredibly resourceful page created by an FSU grad student.

Criminal Justice MegaLinks: Sources of Information on People

http://faculty.ncwc.edu/toconnor/sources.htm

A Web page with links on computer security and computerized databases and how investigators can find out information about anyone.

Cybercrimes

http://www.cybercrimes.net/

An informative site from the University of Dayton Law School.

Electronic Frontier Foundation

http://www.eff.org/

One of the most influential sites on the Internet, it discusses the future of Internet technology and its many promises and pitfalls. Contains special features on government-driven hacker crackdowns.

International Association of Computer Investigative Specialists

http://cops.org/

This is an extensive site produced by an international volunteer nonprofit corporation composed of law enforcement professionals dedicated to education in the field of forensic computer science.

PedoWatch

http://www.pedowatch.org/leinfo/

A citizen safety-oriented comprehensive site on pedophilia and Internet child pornography.

WebGator: Investigative Resources on the Internet

http://www.webgator.org

A site set up by a private investigator with extensive resources for finding anybody.

CORRECTIONS

AZ Prison Reform Committee

http://www.eaznet.com/~jet/

A prison reform site with articles and links on aspects of inmate life, such as the inmate diet and overcrowding.

iSearch: Criminal Justice

Behind the Walls

`http://home.msen.com/~sky1/`

A site put together by a correctional officer in Michigan which deals with controversial issues in corrections, like homosexuality, pepper spray, and privatization. The site also maintains a collection of Internet resources.

Black Peoples' Prison Survival Guide

`http://www.freeworldfriends.com/survivalguide.html`

A Web site featuring an essay written by an ex-convict that claims to tell it like it is about prison and how to survive in it.

Correctional Officer's Information Page

`http://www.geocities.com/MotorCity/Downs/3548/`
`index.html`

A site created by a New York State correctional officer which provides a tremendous number of Internet links on many different correctional topics, specifically issues affecting the unionization of correctional officers.

Corrections Connection Network

`http://www.corrections.com/`

The largest site on the Internet devoted to corrections with vast resources on the topics of technology, education, healthcare, and privatization. It also houses the main prison work professional associations, the American Correctional Association and the American Jail Association.

Corrections/Law Enforcement Connection

`http://members.aol.com/kprior1869`

An AOL home page put together by a correctional sergeant in California that indexes other correctional officer home pages around the nation. The site also offers a multimedia tour of a California prison, other correctional links, miscellaneous links, and a police links page.

Corrections Education Connection

`http://www.ceclibrary.org`

This site provides detailed content on any and all areas affecting the success of education in corrections. There are extensive Internet resources categorized by substance abuse problems, family problems, prison culture

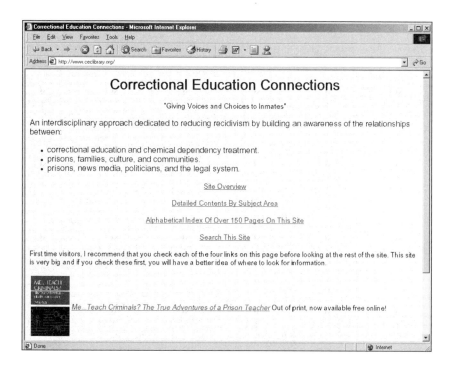

problems, health problems, political problems, and the learning difficulties of inmates.

Criminal Justice Links: Community Corrections and Prisons

`http://www.fsu.edu/~crimdo/prison.html`

Part of a comprehensive site that provides links for community based correctional organizations, community courts, alternative dispute resolution, prison commissions, prison history, prison reform, and death penalty links.

Criminal Justice MegaLinks: Prison and Prison-Related MegaLinks

`http://faculty.ncwc.edu/toconnor/prison.htm`

Part of a comprehensive site that provides links to the Web sites for the prison systems of all fifty states, some federal prisons, and the larger metropolitan jails. Related Internet resources are also listed.

iSearch: Criminal Justice

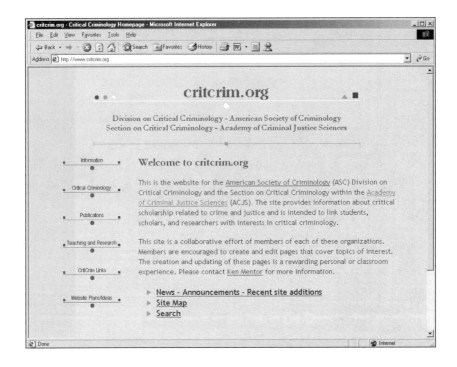

Division of Critical Criminology's Home Page

`http://www.critcrim.org`

An extensive collection of links and original papers on prisons, prison issues, women in prison, prison culture, and prison statistics.

Eastern State Penitentiary

`http://www.libertynet.org/~e-state/`

This is a site that documents the history of the Pennsylvania style penitentiaries in the United States.

History of the North Carolina Prison System

`http://www.doc.state.nc.us/admin/page1.htm`

This site is part of a two-part series of historic photos and commentary showing how the state's prison system evolved from all the way back when prisoners were toted around in horse-drawn cages.

JailNet

http://www.jail.net/

A site with links and resources on issues affecting jail administration, including the law and mandatory jail services. There is a state-by-state directory of jail links.

Jeremy Bentham's Panopticon

http://www.cartome.org/panopticon1.htm

This site explains in both photos and words what Bentham's Panopticon prison's design looked like and was all about.

New Jersey State Parole Board

http://www.state.nj.us/parole/

This site does a good job of explaining the philosophy and operations of a parole board.

New York City Department of Corrections

http://www.ci.nyc.ny.us/html/doc/

The Web site for a system of municipal jails that holds more inmates than some state systems. The site contains history information, archived information, and online newsletters.

New York State Probation Officers Association

http://www.nyspoa.com/

This site does a good job of explaining what a probation officer does.

Prison Issues Desk

http://www.prisonactivist.org/

A site by the Prison Activist Resource Center which contains excellent original resources on the prison crisis, prison law, women prisoners, political prisoners, and prison reform and/or abolition.

Prison Law Page

http://www.wco.com/~aerick/

An informative site dealing with correctional law, inmate rights, the death penalty, and inmate perspectives. The site contains a vocabulary guide to prisoner lingo or jargon as well as a number of other essays and articles.

iSearch: Criminal Justice

Prisons.com

http://www.prisons.com/

A site which features the latest industry products in corrections. It also hosts the online magazine, *Corrections Forum.*

Private Prisons

http://www.ucc.uconn.edu/~logan/

A site put together by a University of Connecticut professor which provides both sides of argument in the privatization of prisons debate.

Web of Justice: Corrections-Related Links

http://www.co.pinellas.fl.us/bcc/juscoord/
ecorrections.htm

Part of a mega-site with a lengthy list of alphabetized Internet resources in corrections. State links are mixed in the list with other links.

Web of Justice: Probation and Parole Links

http://www.co.pinellas.fl.us/bcc/juscoord/
eprobation.htm

Part of a mega-site with a lengthy list of Internet resources in probation and parole. The list is alphabetized by state, but not all states are represented.

COURTS

Administrative Offices of the U.S. Courts

http://www.uscourts.gov/

An exhaustive amount of information on the federal court system.

ADR and Mediation Links

http://adrr.com/

This is a very extensive site on all things related to alternative dispute resolution and mediations, from its philosophy to its actual operations. The site features a topical guide and online essays.

American Judges Association

http://www.ncsc.dni.us/aja/

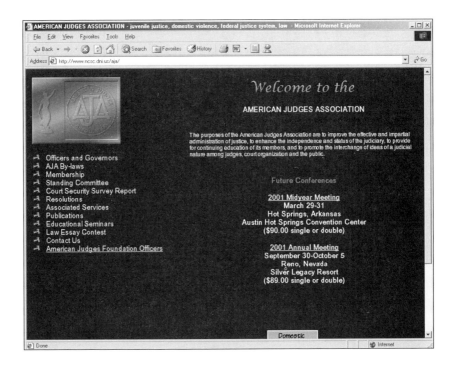

A central clearinghouse of information designed to assist judges and judicial staff. The AJA offers conferences, seminars, and research resources for its member.

Courtroom 21

http://www.courtroom21.net/

A site at College of William and Mary demonstrating the advantages of technology-augmented adjudication and modern courtrooms.

Federal Court Finder

http://www.law.emory.edu/FEDCTS/

An excellent guide to the federal court system from Emory University Law School.

Gwinnett Judicial Circuit

http://www.gwinnettcourts.com

This site in Georgia gives a great overview of superior courts and courts of limited jurisdiction.

iSearch: Criminal Justice

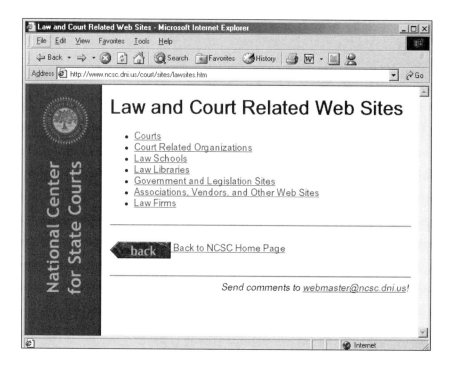

Law and Court-Related Web sites

`http://www.ncsc.dni.us/court/sites/lawsites.htm`

This site includes links to legal institutions of all kinds, including courts, law schools, law libraries, governments, legislatures, and law firms. It is an excellent starting point for researching the judicial process.

National Association for Court Management

`http://www.nacmnet.org/`

This site includes links to court-related Web sites, an online newsletter, and other publications on how to more effectively manage the courts to improve public access to them.

National Center for the State Courts

`http://www.ncsonline.org`

An exhaustive amount of information on state court systems.

Oyez Oyez Oyez

http://oyez.nwu.edu/

This is a multimedia-enriched site with excellent information about the U.S. Supreme Court. It also briefs key cases and analyzes oral arguments.

Redwood Highway: Law and Court Links

http://www.sonoma.edu/cja/info/infop3.html

Part of a mega-site with an annotated guide to legal sites. The bottom of the page focuses exclusively on California.

Serious Criminal Defense Litigation

http://www.execpc.com/~wrfincke/

A seasoned lawyer tells it like it is about defending clients. The site defines the role of the lawyer, the adversarial system, and more.

State Justice Institute

http://www.statejustice.org/

The SJI award grants to improve the quality of justice in the state court systems facilitate better coordination and information sharing, and to foster innovative, efficient solutions to common problems faced by all courts.

CRIME ANALYSIS

Crime Mapping and Analysis

http://everest.hunter.cuny.edu/capse/projects/
nij/crime.html

This is a site put together by a government researcher to post the results of his research. The result is a site that offers practical explanations and suggestions for getting started with GIS or geographic mapping.

Criminal Justice MegaLinks: Data Sources in Criminal Justice

http://faculty.ncwc.edu/toconnor/data.htm

A site put together by a college professor for students to learn about how and where to collect crime-related data, arranged by topic.

iSearch: Criminal Justice

International Association of Crime Analysts

http://www.iaca.net/

This association has an extensive and useful Web site. The site includes tutorials on crime mapping, what crime analysis is, a list of job openings, a newsletter, and related links of interest.

Tempe (AZ) Police Department Crime Analysis Unit

http://www.tempe.gov/cau/default.htm

Informative site about police analysis of crime data.

CRIME LABS AND FORENSIC SCIENCE

Anil Aggrawal's Forensic Toxicology Page

http://members.tripod.com/~Prof_Anil_Aggrawal/

This is an interesting site from India on various topics in forensic medicine, with links to other Internet resources. It contains an online journal.

Carpenter's Forensic Science Links

http://www.tncrimlaw.com/forensic/

This extensive site offers excellent resources in forensic anthropology, pathology, entomology, odontology, document examination, and crime scene investigation. There's also information on education in forensic science.

Forensic Psychiatry and Medicine

http://www.forensic-psych.com/articles/
catCrimJust.html

This site contains excellent articles on the evidentiary rules of forensic science, as well as explaining the difference between diminished capacity defenses and insanity defenses.

Forensic Psychiatry Resource Page

http://bama.ua.edu/~jhooper/

A large and useful site on the variety of services offered by a psychologist or psychiatrist in law. It explains a bit about getting at the *mens rea* requirement.

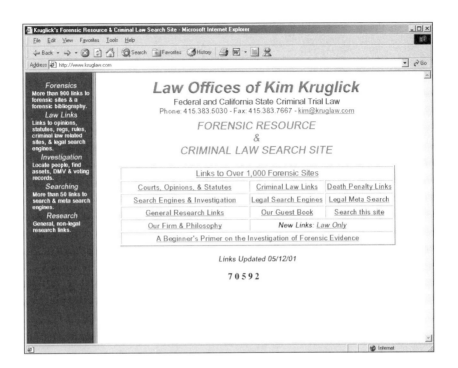

Forensic Resource and Criminal Law Search Site

http://www.kruglaw.com/

A large and extremely useful site with over 900 forensic science, criminal law, and death penalty resources.

Fraud Detection

http://www.forensicpage.com/

Links to and about the whole areas of lie detection, document examination, handwriting analysis, and fraud detection.

Knowledge Solutions

http://www.corpus-delicti.com/

A site that sells online courses in forensic science and psychological profiling. Some of the content is free, however, and the resources are quite good. Topics include computer crime and serial killing.

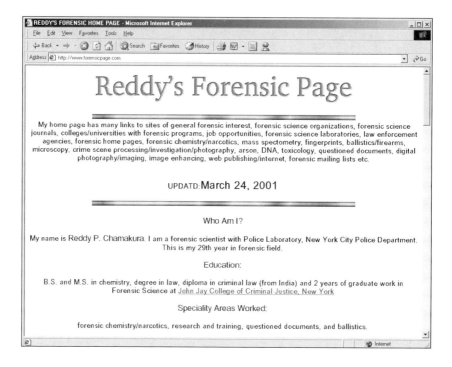

Michigan State Police Forensic Science Division

`http://members.aol.com/stevenkl/fsdhome2.htm`

A well-done page with exhaustive depth of content in DNA fingerprinting, ballistics, and other topics. It also contains links to other forensic crime labs around the country.

Reddy's Forensic Science Links

`http://www.forensicpage.com`

This is one of the premier forensic science sites on the Internet. It has dozens of pages on just about any kind of forensic science imaginable.

Reference Manual on Scientific Evidence

`http://www.fjc.gov/EVIDENCE/science/sc_ev_sec.html`

A lengthy and detailed account of the evidentiary standards for all the different types of forensic science from federal government guidelines.

Study Guides in Forensic Science

http://www.msu.edu/user/siegelj/

Study guides and notes provided online by a Michigan State University professor.

Zeno's Forensic Page

http://forensic.to/forensic.html

This is one of the premier forensic science sites on the Internet. Although all types of forensic science are represented, the site concentrates on medical, psychiatric, and psychological specialties.

CRIME NEWS

About.com: Current Events—Civil Liberties

http://civilliberty.about.com/newsissues/
civilliberty/

A site that "mines" the Internet for the best stories about civil liberties.

About.com: Current Events—Crime/Punishment

http://crime.about.com/newsissues/crime/

A site that "mines" the Internet for the best stories about crime.

About.com: Current Events—Law

http://law.about.com/newsissues/law/

A site that "mines" the Internet for the best stories about law.

APB Online

http://www.apbonline.com/

A multimedia site devoted mainly to the unsolved crimes genre.

Court TV Online

http://www.courttv.com/

An extensively resourceful site that focuses upon the latest trials, crime stories, and pros and cons.

iSearch: Criminal Justice

Criminal Justice MegaLinks: Current Events

http://faculty.ncwc.edu/toconnor/current.htm

A site put together by a college professor with links to the top news stories arranged in an alphabetical list of topics.

CyberSleuth's Crime News

http://www.cybersleuths.com/

A site that scans the nation's newspapers for top stories.

Policy News

http://www.policy.com/

A portion of speakout.com that focuses on events and decisions with important policy implications.

Yahoo's Coverage of Correction and Rehabilitation

http://dir.yahoo.com/society_and_culture/crime/
correction_and_Rehabilitation/News_and_Media

A site that indexes a variety of online publications covering topics from the world of corrections.

CRIME PREVENTION

National Crime Prevention Council

http://www.ncpc.org/

Home of McGruff the Crime Dog and other resources on crime prevention.

Security Management Online

http://www.securitymanagement.com/

An online magazine and extensive resource site on the many areas of private security.

CRIMINAL JUSTICE EDUCATION

Complete Criminal Justice, Criminology, and Criminal Law Glossary

http://talkjustice.com/files/glossary.htm

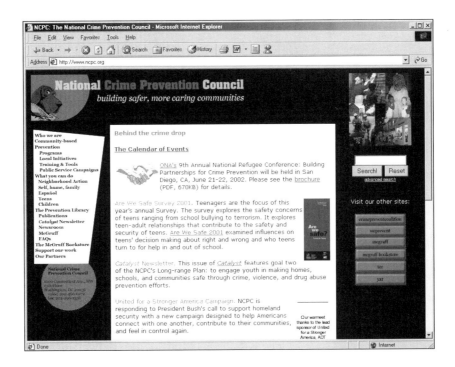

This site contains every possible term you would need to know in criminology and criminal justice. The searchable database gives the definitions of over 1,000 terms, from Administrative Law to White Collar Crime.

Crime Connections on the Web: Criminal Justice Education in the U.S.

http://www.appstate.edu/~robinsnmb/education.htm

A professor at Appalachain State University put together this listing of undergraduate and graduate programs, arranged alphabetically.

Criminal Justice Links: Criminal Justice Education

http://www.criminology.fsu.edu/cjlinks/cjed.html

A professor at Florida State University put together this listing of graduate and undergraduate programs. It includes training institutes, continuing legal education, entry tests, and job searches.

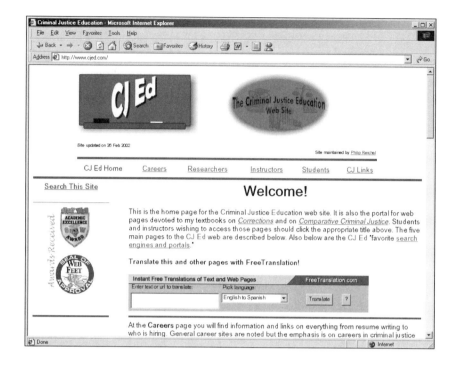

Graduate Schools in Criminal Justice: A State-by-State Guide

http://faculty.ncwc.edu/toconnor/jusgrad.htm

A professor at North Carolina Wesleyan College put together this listing of all master's and doctoral degree programs. It includes a sample curriculum.

Phil Reichel's Criminal Justice Education Page

http://www.cjed.com/

A professor at the University of Northern Colorado put together this site to assist both criminal justice students and professors.

CRIMINAL JUSTICE EMPLOYMENT

Criminal Justice MegaLinks: Employment MegaLinks

http://faculty.ncwc.edu/toconnor/employ.htm

A site put together by a professor for his students and others as a guide to obtaining employment in criminal justice fields. The site offers original content as well as an extensive collection of Internet resources.

LeoLinks: Employment

`http://www.leolinks.com/employment/`

An extensive jobs page from a mega-site in policing. Résumé-posting is allowed, and there are career guides online.

www.Officer.com: Law Enforcement Recruiting Directory

`http://www.officer.com/recruiting/index.htm`

The jobs page from the most popular Web site in law enforcement. There are federal jobs listed and the rest of the page is organized state-by-state.

CRIMINAL JUSTICE HISTORY

The Crime Library

`http://www.crimelibrary.com/`

A site with factual and fictionalized accounts of famous criminals, serial killers, gangsters, spies, and assassins.

Criminal Justice History Resources

`http://arapaho.nsuok.edu/~dreveskr/cjhr.html-ssi`

A professor at Northeastern State University (Oklahoma) put together this amazing collection of links arranged by historical time periods.

CRIMINAL JUSTICE PROCEDURE

Anatomy of a Prosecution

`http://www.co.eaton.mi.us/ecpa/process.htm`

This is one of the best criminal justice sites on the Internet. It takes you step-by-step through all the processes, from arrest to final appeal.

APA Division 41's Psychology and Law Links

`http://www.unl.edu/ap-ls/`

A collection of psychology and law links from this group of psychologists interested in law.

Admissibility of Scientific Evidence under Daubert

`http://faculty.ncwc.edu/toconnor/daubert.htm`

An essay and informative article on what weight should be placed on various types of evidence, like fingerprinting, DNA, voice analysis, and so forth.

iSearch: Criminal Justice

Criminal Defense Online

http://www.sado.org/

A site that explains the basics of the criminal justice system from a know-your-rights perspective. Contains samples and illustrations of various documents, such as presentence investigative reports, legal briefs, and requests for information under the Freedom of Information Act.

Effective Search and Seizure

http://www.fsu.edu/~crimdo/fagan.html

An online essay by a Florida State University professor which delves into the details of probable cause.

Evidence Site

http://www.law.umich.edu/thayer/

A site constructed by and mostly for lawyers to better understand the changes in evidence law. Contains newsletters, conference reports, recommended readings, and some suggested links.

Expert Testimony on Eyewitness Reliability

http://www.sado.org/19cdn12.htm#19cdn12a

An online essay that explains quite a bit about eyewitness testimony, the errors associated with it, and how experts can either bolster or destroy the testimony of an eyewitness.

FAQs about Grand Juries

http://www.udayton.edu/~grandjur/

This is one of the best resources on the Internet for information about juries in general and grand juries in particular.

Format of a Criminal Trial

http://faculty.ncwc.edu/toconnor/trialfrm.htm

This site contains a summary table and extensive, real-life descriptions of the steps in a criminal trial.

Fully Informed Jury Association

http://nowscape.com/fija/fija_us.htm

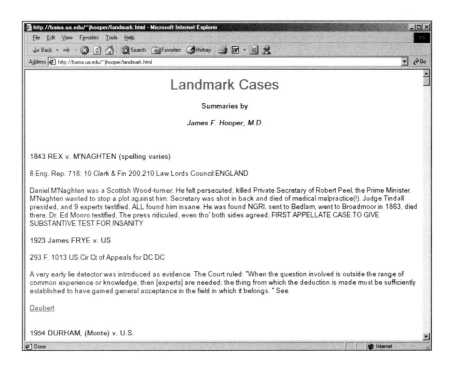

This is an excellent source of information on the Internet. The site covers issues such as jury reform, jury nullification, and the image of justice on television shows.

Handbook for Trial Jurors

http://www.ncmd.uscourts.gov/jurhbook.htm

An extensive and practical guide to everything a jury is supposed to do.

Landmark Cases in Psychiatry and Law

http://ua1vm.ua.edu/~jhooper/landmark.html

This sites explores the landmark cases that added things like competency to stand trial and insanity to criminal procedure.

Legal Survival Guide

http://www.courttv.com/legalhelp/lawguide/criminal/

This is an excellent site that walks you through, step-by-step, all the stages of criminal procedure, from affidavit to appeal. The topics of pretrial procedures are covered as well as trial procedures.

iSearch: Criminal Justice

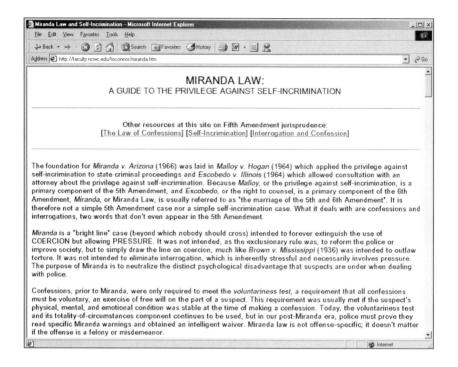

Miranda Law: A Guide to the Privilege against Self-Incrimination

http://faculty.ncwc.edu/toconnor/miranda.htm

A site that provides extensive detail on the Miranda warnings that police officers should give you.

Nolo Press

http://www.nolo.com/

A publishing company's site that provides a number of online resources and self-help guides for people in trouble with the law.

Online Directory of Expert Witnesses

http://www.claims.com/

A site where different experts from around the country have deposited their resumes in hopes that someone trying a case could use their services.

Pardon Me: The Pardon Resource Center

http://www.silicon-valley.com/pardonme/index.shtml

A site that focuses exclusively on pardons, executive clemency, expungements, and so forth.

PreTrial Professionals of Florida

http://www.appf.org

A comprehensive law site focusing exclusively on pretrial procedures such as the filing of affidavits and motions in the state of Florida.

Scientific Testimony: Tutorials

http://www.scientific.org/tutorials/tutorial.html

This site, part of an online journal, contains articles on DNA testing and DNA exonerations which are written in laymen's terms.

Search and Seizure: A Guide to Rules, Requirements, Tests, Doctrines, and Special Circumstances

http://faculty.ncwc.edu/toconnor/serchrul.htm

A site that provides extensive detail on searches and seizures by the police.

TnCrimLaw

http://www.tncrimlaw.com/

Part of Carpenter's site in forensic science, TnCrimLaw on this page has a section called Explanations in Everyday Language which contains concise explanations of key criminal justice procedures, like What is an Arraignment? What is a Preliminary Hearing? What is a Grand Jury? There's even an online glossary of terms in criminal justice.

CRIMINAL JUSTICE REFORM

Children's Defense Fund

http://www.childrensdefense.org/

An influential lobby group devoted to being the voice for all children in America. Their Web site contains information about the stands they take on important issues affecting children's rights, such as those involving being a victim of crime.

iSearch: Criminal Justice

Citizens United for the Rehabilitation of Errants

http://www.curenational.org/index.html

CURE is an advocacy and lobby organization for the reduction of crime through criminal law reform. It opposes capital punishment and control units, favoring instead more use of education and programs. Their Web site offers original and Internet resources.

Criminal Justice MegaLinks: A Glossary of Social Reforms

http://faculty.ncwc.edu/toconnor/reform.htm

An online, hyperlinked encyclopedia with listings from A to Z on every social experiment or feat of social engineering tried in the late twentieth century to fight crime, fight poverty, and improve society.

Families against Mandatory Minimums

http://www.famm.org/

This nonprofit organization, which claims that the criminal justice system is broken, proposes and documents extensively the reasons why mandatory minimum sentences should be abolished. The site offers original and Internet resources on sentencing reform.

Freedom Forum

http://www.freedomforum.org/

This is a First Amendment watchdog group with information on their site about free speech, press, religion, and assembly.

Howard League for Penal Reform

http://web.ukonline.co.uk/howard.league/

Based in the United Kingdom, this charity organization, founded by John Howard, has historical importance. Their site offers a number of original publications and has an extensive collection of Internet resource links on many different aspects of penal reform.

Injustice Line

http://home.earthlink.net/~ynot/

A Web site dedicated to exposing and publicizing injustices. One of the features at this site is a list of twelve justice system reforms.

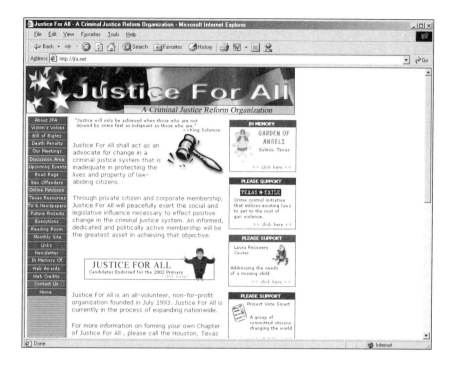

Justice for All

`http://www.jfa.net/`

A victims-oriented reform group with a pro-death penalty stance.

Koch Crime Institute

`http://www.kci.org/`

A nonprofit organization that studies the criminal and juvenile justice system in an effort to reduce crime, especially juvenile crime. Their site has a juvenile boot camp directory, a collection of links on methamphetamine use, and resources on the privatization of prisons.

National Urban League

`http://www.nul.org`

A group to assist African Americans in the achievement of social and economic equality.

The Stop Violence Project

http://stopviolence.com

A site put together by students at Eastern Michigan University on school violence, hate crime, and violence prevention.

Peacemaking and Crime

http://www.westga.edu/~jfuller/peace.html

Professor John Fuller's site at University of West Georgia is an excellent resource on various alternative justice systems.

Prison Activist Resource Center

http://www.prisonactivist.org/

The extensive site has a number of resources on prison reform.

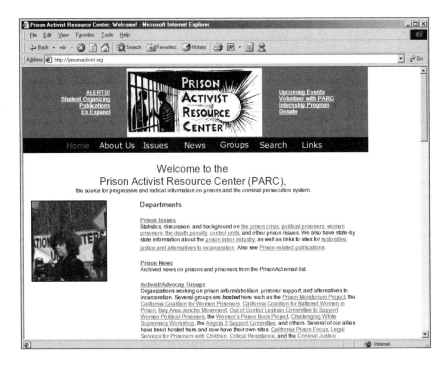

RAND

http://www.rand.org/

A public policy think tank with online resources in criminal justice policy analysis, drugs and crime, immigration and crime, sentencing, drug control, and violence reduction. The site contains copies of recent publications and newsletters.

Redwood Highway: System Critique and Reform

http://www.sonoma.edu/cja/info/infop6.html

Part of a mega-site with essays and links on alternative and progressive thoughts about the criminal justice system.

Sentencing Project

http://www.sentencingproject.org/

The Sentencing Project is an independent source of policy analysis and information for the public about sentencing. They support the Campaign for an Effective Crime Policy, and their site has extensive resources on school violence, boot camps, drug courts, mandatory minimums, and the relationship between imprisonment and the crime rate.

Stop Prisoner Rape

http://www.igc.org/spr/

A nonprofit organization with their Web site hosted on IGC that takes an activist stance toward ending the prison and jailhouse rapes of prisoners. They provide extensive news coverage and other features on their site.

True Justice to the Unjust

http://members.tripod.com/~MerlM/index.html

An angry kind of site that is posting every known instance in the news about crimes by the police, judicial misconduct, and correctional abuses.

Vera Institute of Justice

http://www.vera.org/

A nonprofit think tank that is devoted to finding creative and innovative alternatives to punishment like imprisonment. The Vera Institute has conducted research on jury reform and appearance in court, two areas where they make their studies public on their Web site. The Vera Institute Web site also has an excellent collection of justice-related Internet resources.

iSearch: Criminal Justice

CRIMINOLOGY

Australian Institute of Criminology

http://www.aic.gov.au/

An extensive site that reviews the worldwide criminological literature for possible policy applications in Australia and elsewhere.

Crime Magazine

http://www.crimemagazine.com/

An online publishing venue which covers mostly celebrity crime, serial crime, sex crime, and organized crime.

CrimeTheory.com

http://www.crimetheory.com/

A site created by Prof. Bruce Hoffman at the University of Washington which contains extensive resources on criminological theories and theorists.

Crime Times

http://www.crime-times.org/

An online newsletter and other resources specifically devoted to biological theories and research into the causes of criminal behavior.

Criminal Justice MegaLinks: Criminology

http://faculty.ncwc.edu/toconnor/criminology.htm

An academic site put together by a professor to explain criminological theory, motives for crime underlying the theories, and policy implications.

Criminal Psychology

http://www.geocities.com/CapitolHill/Lobby/6027/

This site contains serious and amusing resources on the psychological causes of criminal behavior.

Criminological Theory

http://people.ne.mediaone.net/dianedemelo/crime/crimetheory.html

This is a site which was created by Professor Diane DeMelo which outlines the major theories in criminology, some of which have active links which lead to a fuller explanation of the theory.

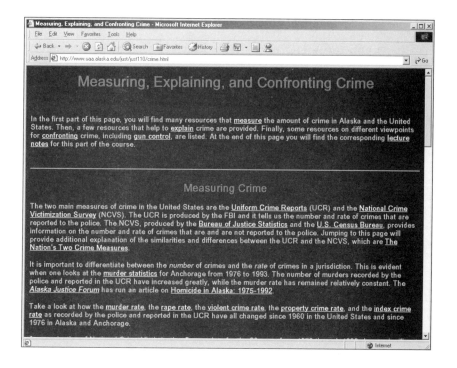

Critical Criminology Division Home Page

http://www.criterim.org

An academic site with extensive resources on restorative justice, peace-making criminology, the death penalty, gun control, wrongful conviction, and more.

Measuring, Explaining, and Confronting Crime

http://local.uaa.alaska.edu/~afdsw/crime.html

A professor at the University of Alaska put this site together to explain how crime is measured, explained, and confronted using various Internet resources as hyperlinks in the sentences.

Rational Criminals and Intentional Accidents

http://www.best.com/~ddfr/Academic/Hidden_Order/ Hidden_Order_Chapter_20.html

An economic point of view on law breaking.

Sociological Theories of Deviance

`http://www.d.umn.edu/~jhamlin1/soc3305.html`

This is a site created by Professor John Hamlin at the University of Minnesota which provides notes on various sociological explanations for crime.

Sociological Tour through HyperSpace: Theories

`http://www.trinity.edu/~mkearl/theory.html`

An excellent collection of Internet resource links on sociological theories.

SocioRealm: Criminology

`http://www.digeratiweb.com/sociorealm`

This excellent and resourceful site has a section on criminology which includes links to all sorts of papers and articles on criminological theory, adult and juvenile violence, corporate crime, and criminal justice links.

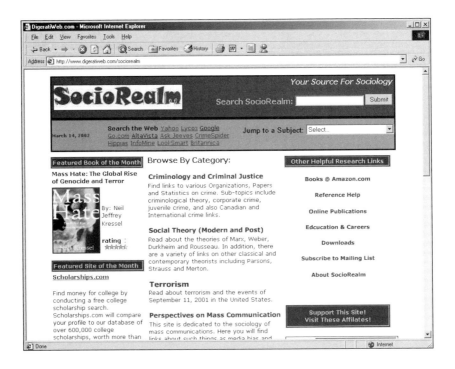

Solon's Voyage

http://www.geocities.com/Athens/Acropolis/7001/

This site, located in Australia, is an excellent resource for everything about women and law, women and criminology, and sentencing from a woman's perspective.

Western Society of Criminology

http://www.sonoma.edu/cja/wsc/wscmain.html

Actually two sites in one, this URL provides you with online newsletter and journal articles about crime and criminological theory.

DEATH PENALTY

Anti-Death Penalty Resources

http://sun.soci.niu.edu/~critcrim/dp/dp.html

An excellent resource site from the ASC Division of Critical Criminology. Includes statistics from recent years, fact sheets, Supreme Court decisions, and generalized and specific links.

Death Penalty Information Center

http://www.deathpenaltyinfo.org/

A fact-filled site useful for research on race, women, juveniles, the mentally retarded, and capital punishment.

Death Penalty Links

http://www.derechos.org/dp/

A lengthy collection of links and original essays from the Derechos Human Rights Campaign.

Death Penalty News

http://www.smu.edu/~deathpen/

An online newsletter that tracks scheduled executions by name and state. Other Internet resource links are provided.

iSearch: Criminal Justice

Death, Reason, and Judgment: The American Experience

`http://lgxserver.uniba.it/lei/filpol/allen.htm`

An interesting commentary that argues against getting tough on crime from a financial or economic point of view.

ElectricChair.com

`http://www.theelectricchair.com/`

A rather shocking site that focuses upon the history of electrocution and answers almost every question imaginable about it.

Fatal Flaws: Innocence and the Death Penalty

`http://www.amnesty.org/802568F7005C4453/0/`
`D68742CD70EE65678025690000692F0B?Open`

A lengthy 1998 article from Amnesty International, significant for its superb investigative research on inmates who were executed but later found innocent.

Professor David's Death Penalty Resources

`http://www.uncp.edu/home/vanderhoof/death.html`

A professor put this site together to stimulate critical thinking about the death penalty. It organizes Internet resources in an interesting way.

Punishment and the Death Penalty

`http://ethics.acusd.edu/death_penalty.html`

This site contains discussion and links about punishment in general and the death penalty in particular.

DRUGS

PREVLINE: Prevention Online

`http://www.health.org`

Resources and online data on federal, state, and local anti-drug initiatives. A good starting place for drug researchers.

National Drug Prevention League

`http://www.ndpl.org/`

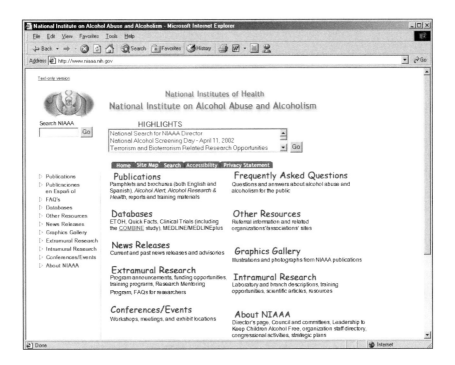

An association of private sector organizations for drug abuse prevention. The site provides links to Internet resources and information, including national surveys and studies, federal programs, and proposed legislation.

National Institute of Alcohol Abuse and Alcoholism

http://www.niaaa.nih.gov/

A division of the National Institute of Health which was constructed to combat alcohol problems by providing reports about them.

National Institute of Drug Abuse

http://www.nida.nih.gov

A division of the National Institute of Health which contains much of the research that is known about drug abuse and addiction.

Partnership for a Drug-Free America

http://www.drugfreeamerica.org/

This site has a comprehensive database of drug information, what to do, what drugs look like, their history, and slang terms.

Policing for Profit: The Drug War's Hidden Economic Agenda

http://www.fear.org/chicago.html

A rather lengthy, but important, paper on the policies of asset forfeiture and using R.I.C.O. statutes to confiscate the defendant's property.

Reddy's Forensic Links: Forensic Chemistry/Narcotics

http://haven.ios.com/~nyrc/new15.htm

Part of a mega-site in forensic science that focuses upon drugs, drug interactions, and what the experts say in terms of how it influences criminal behavior.

Ultimate Drug Links Resource

http://www.algonet.se/~birdy/druglink/

An alphabetical listing of every drug known throughout history.

Web of Addictions

http://www.well.com/user/woa/

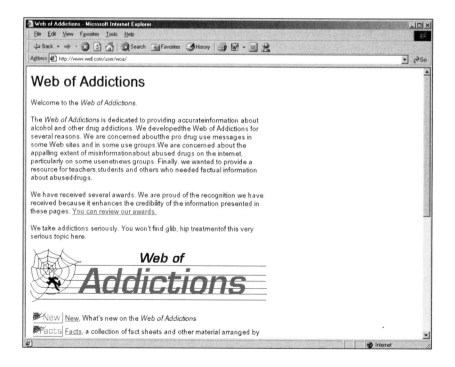

A site dedicated to providing accurate information about alcohol and other drugs as a resource for teachers, students, and others who need factual information about abused drugs and addictive behavior.

GANGS AND JUVENILE CRIME

American Bar Associations Juvenile Justice Center

`http://www.abanet.org/crimjust/juvjus/home.html`

A special feature Web site with online publications, articles, and links on juvenile justice and the special due process safeguards therein.

Florida State's Juvenile Delinquency and Juvenile Justice Links

`http://www.criminology.fsu.edu/cjlinks/jd.html`

One of Florida State's research centers, the site explains what research they carry out, and what policy recommendations they have made.

Gang and Security Threat Group Awareness

`http://www.dc.state.fl.us/pub/gangs/index.html`

A site provided by the Florida Department of Corrections that is about prison gangs in Florida and elsewhere. It provides extensive information about the history, symbols, and identifiers for at least six major gangs, including Chicago-based and L.A.-based ones. There's also a guide to basic facts about gangs and answers to frequently asked questions.

Juvenile Boot Camp Directory

`http://www.kci.org/publication/bootcamp/`
`prerelease.htm`

A page from the Koch Crime Institute site which shows a map of the nation's juvenile boot camps. There are additional links on the page from government publications on boot camps.

Juvenile Justice Home Page

`http://www.edwardhumes.com/links.htm#juvenile`

This site provides excellent resources on the history of the juvenile court and links to contemporary research reports.

iSearch: Criminal Justice

LeoLinks: Gang Links

http://www.leolinks.com/search/
Intelligence_Crime_Stats/Gangs/index.shtml

A long list of gang links of interest to police officers.

Midwest Gang Investigators Association

http://www.mgia.org

A page created by a correctional officer which offers extensive resources on gang definitions, gang activities, guides to Midwest gangs, recommended readings, and links to other state gang investigation sites.

National Youth Gang Center

http://www.iir.com/nygc/

This Center assists state and local governments in the collection, analysis, and exchange of information on gang-related demographics, legislation, literature, research, and promising strategies. It is an excellent resource for gang researchers.

NCJRS Index of Juvenile Justice Documents

http://virlib.ncjrs.org/JuvenileJustice.asp

Online documents from this government information clearinghouse.

Street Gang Dynamics

http://www.gangwar.com/dynamics.htm

A free, online book from gangwar.com that is worth reading in its entirety as a beginner's manual on understanding street gangs, their motivations, and graffiti interpretation.

HUMAN RIGHTS

American Civil Liberties Union

http://www.aclu.org/

An organizational lobby site that serves as a legal defense resource for various civil rights groups, including immigrants, gays and lesbians, minorities, and victims of discrimination. It has extensive resources on free speech, cyberliberties, and criminal justice issues.

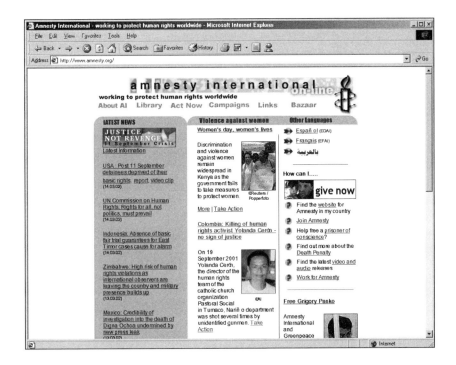

Amnesty International

`http://www.amnesty.org/`

An international watchdog group that documents criminal justice system incidents of torture, brutality, and violations of human rights.

Directory of Human Rights Resources on the Internet

`http://shr.aaas.org/dhr.htm`

A huge collection of human rights-related resources, indexed topically and geographically.

Human Rights Watch Prison Project

`http://www.hrw.org/advocacy/prisons/index.htm`

Part of the Human Rights Web (**http://www.hrweb.org/**), this site is dedicated to ending the abusive treatment of prisoners. Human Rights Watch has conducted specialized prison research and helped to focus international attention on prison conditions worldwide. Their site details the most common abuses inflicted on prisoners.

iSearch: Criminal Justice

IGC Network

http://www.igc.org/igc/

The largest political activist site on the Internet that includes extensive resources on women and crime, race and crime, and social justice.

National Civil Rights Museum

http://www.civilrightsmuseum.org

A multimedia tour of the civil rights movement.

LAW

Constitution Notebook Program

http://members.aol.com/tcnbp/

The owner of this site wants to sell his Constitutional Law guide to you, but most of his site is freely accessible. This sites makes for an excellent Constitutional Law source. Almost every line in the Constitution is analyzed word-for-word.

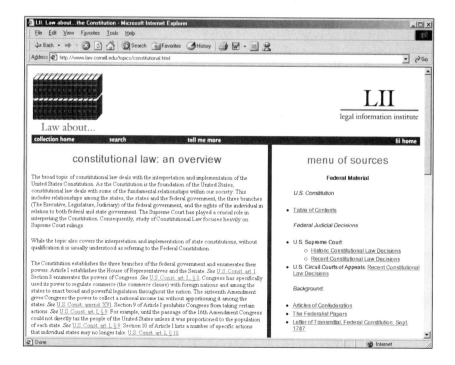

Constitutional Law: An Overview

`http://www.law.cornell.edu/topics/constitutional.html`

The simplest and most concise summary of the whole field of Constitutional Law on the Internet, from Cornell's Legal Information Institute.

Criminal Justice Links: Searchable Law Databases

`http://www.fsu.edu/~crimdo/law.html`

This page has an extensive listing of law links, but its main feature is its annotated listing of the various legal research search engines.

Criminal Justice MegaLinks: Mega-Guide to Law and Law Schools

`http://faculty.ncwc.edu/toconnor/megalaw.htm`

This page provides links and essays on different types of law, what it's like to study the law, and has a comprehensive list of all Law Schools in the United States with their entry requirements.

Duhaime's Legal Dictionary

`http://www.duhaime.org/diction.htm`

An online legal dictionary, written free of charge, by a lawyer.

FindLaw

`http://www.findlaw.com/`

An easy-to-use legal search engine with topical guides.

Five Hour Law School

`http://members.aol.com/ronin48th/hope.htm`

A site that explains in five hours everything that a lawyer is trained in and what lawyers do. There's an online glossary of terms, but the best feature is the explanation of which of those books in the library to use first.

Hieros Gamos: The Comprehensive Law Site

`http://www.hg.org/`

A large site covering many different areas of law from all over the world.

Law Guru

http://www.lawguru.com/

An "ask-the-expert" site with previously posted questions and answers.

Law and Politics Internet Guide

http://www.geocities.com/CapitolHill/Lobby/5011/

A site designed for one-stop shopping in your legal research needs. You can use the topical guides to things like death penalty resources, or there's an extremely flexible search engine.

Law School Admissions Council

http://www.lsac.org/

This is the site for the organization that administers the LSAT entry exam for law schools. It has extensive resources, including sample exams and financial aid help pages.

Legal Information Institute

http://www.law.cornell.edu/

This site at Cornell University is widely regarded as the best site on the Internet for law. There are topical guides to the law in common areas like the Constitution, Criminal Law, and Criminal Procedure. All of the U.S. Codes as well as all recent and historical Supreme Court cases are online and searchable by number or by name. Opinions of the Appeals courts are also online.

Legal Research Online

http://www.galaxy.com/galaxy/Government/Law.html

There's an assortment of resources at this site, featuring mostly examples of different forms used in the practice of law.

State Laws on the Internet

http://www.megalaw.com/

This site provides links to every state at which the criminal law can be looked up, commentary and comparisons can be found, and legal research can almost be conducted.

WashLaw Web: Washburn University School of Law

http://www.washlaw.edu/

An extensive and well-organized set of state law links.

Web Guide to the Constitution

http://tcnbp.tripod.com/webguid.htm

A short, but complete, section-by-section and amendment-by-amendment analysis of the Constitution.

POLICE

911 Theory and Operations

http://www.the911site.com

An excellent site that explains everything you would want to know about 911 emergency services.

Broken Windows

http://www.theatlantic.com/unbound/flashbks/crime/
crime.htm

The web reposting of an early, influential article called "Broken Windows," written by James Q. Wilson and George Kelling at this *Atlantic Monthly* Flashbacks site.

Carolina's Institute for Community Policing

http://www.cicp.org/

A research center and institute with numerous reports and essays online about the more high-tech end of community policing.

Community Policing Consortium

http://www.communitypolicing.org/

A site with online lectures and other training materials to learn about the many aspects of community policing.

Community Policing Pages

http://www.concentric.net/~dwoods/tribute.htm

A tribute site to the founder of community policing, Robert Trojanowicz. The site also contains horror stories of community policing gone wrong.

iSearch: Criminal Justice

CopLink

http://www.coplink.com/copops.htm

This is a site about the basic functions of law enforcement, such as patrol work, traffic safety, and detective work.

Exposing Police Racism

http://www.bwbadge.com/

A site dedicated to exposing and combatting police racism and corruption.

Fighting Police Abuse

http://www.aclu.org/library/fighting_police_abuse.html

An extensive Web site put together by the ACLU to expose and combat police brutality and police spying.

History of the Berkeley Police Department

http://www.ci.berkeley.ca.us/police/history/history.html

A site that details the history of this department and its influential police chief and famous police reformer, August Vollmer.

History of the Metropolitan Police Service

http://www.met.police.uk/police/mps/history/index.htm

A site that chronicles the origin of the London "Bobbies" and their founder, Sir Robert Peel.

History of the Pennsylvania State Police

http://www.state.pa.us/PA_Exec/State_Police/history/history.htm

A site about what history regards as the first professional state police.

Law Enforcement Links on the Web

http://www.ih2000.net/ira/ira.htm

A mega-site with thousands of police links, arranged on big pages.

Law Enforcement Online

http://www.pima.edu/dps/police.htm

This is an excellent and fairly complete collection of law enforcement agencies with Web sites.

LawSearch: The Police Officer's Search Engine

http://www.copscgi.com/

This site has an extremely well-organized database and site layout. You can search for topics such as police humor or technology. There are sections of the site for downloading shareware and for entering a chat room.

CopSeek.com

http://www.leolinks.com/

One of the largest sites in policing, CopSeek categorizes resources by type of police operation, type of agency, and type of crime. There is an extensive array of other resources, including mailing lists and discussion forums.

Miami Metro-Dade Police Department

http://www.mdpd.com

An example of a consolidated, city-county police department.

Nassau County (NY) Police Department

http://www.co.nassau.ny.us/police/index.html

One of the nation's largest county police departments.

Official Directory of State Patrol and State Police

http://www.statetroopersdirectory.com

A directory of all state police departments in the United States.

New York City Police Department

http://www.ci.nyc.ny.us/html/nypd/home.html

The largest municipal police department in the United States.

Organization of the Royal Canadian Mounted Police

http://www.rcmp-grc.gc.ca/html/organiz.htm

An excellent Web site with tons of information about the RCMP.

iSearch: Criminal Justice

PIMA's List of Military Police Departments Online

http://www.pima.edu/dps/Mil.htm

A collection of military police Web sites.

Police Guide

http://www.policeguide.com/

A large site in policing which tends to be focused on collectibles, but there are other interesting online resources in the way of memorabilia and a good guide to cop culture.

Police and Policing

http://local.uaa.alaska.edu/~afdsw/police.html

An online, hyperlink essay about policing from this University of Alaska professor's site.

Police Brutality and Excessive Force

http://web.amnesty.org/802568F7005C4453/
016D4EA481BABB55B28025690000693100?Open

A report from Amnesty International on the New York City police department.

Police Officer Stress and Agency Structure

http://www.ifip.com/acjs1rr.htm

An interesting article about the inherent stresses of police work.

Police Stress Line

http://www.geocities.com/~halbrown/index4.html

A site containing original articles and other content dealing exclusively with various topics in the area of police stress. The author of this Web site is a police stress therapist.

Police Structure of the United States

http://faculty.ncwc.edu/toconnor/polstruct.htm

An online essay and directory of links for federal, state, county, and municipal police departments.

Small Town and Rural Crime Page

http://www.ilstu.edu/depts/cjs/rural.htm

An online bibliography and collection of essays about small town policing and how it's different from big city policing.

Status of Women in Policing

http://www.feminist.org/police/default.asp

A comprehensive site reporting the status of women in policing and containing several other essays or sources of information on issues related to women and policing, including the police family.

Texas Ranger's Hall of Fame and Museum

http://www.texasranger.org/

A site that tells the history of the first state police force.

www.Officer.com

http://www.officer.com/

The largest directory of police departments and their special units on the Internet.

REHABILITATION

Drama Therapy in Criminal Justice

http://www.geesetheatre.com

This site claims that by using psychodrama and other performing art techniques, many criminal offenders can be rehabilitated.

Institute of Behavioral Research

http://www.ibr.tcu.edu/projects/crimjust/pta.html

An Institute at Texas Christian University which is dedicated full-time to the study of substance abuse treatment issues in prison. Their site has project reports, recidivism studies, and a newsletter.

National Institute for the Psychotherapies

http://www.nipinst.org/

A group that conducts training programs to enhance the development of mental health treatment skills.

PsychWeb

http://www.psychwww.com/

An exhaustive site on all aspects of psychology and particularly strong in the area of abnormal psychology.

Psychology Information Online

http://www.psychologyinfo.com/

An extensive site with excellent resources in forensic psychology and applications of psychology to diagnosis and treatment of problems relating to criminal behavior or being a victim of crime.

Reducing Recidivism: What Works?

http://www.bestweb.net/~cureny/

Online articles that contain scholarly reviews of the research summarizing much of what we know about rehabilitating prisoners.

Treatment of Violent Offenders

http://www.csc-scc.gc.ca/text/publicsubject_e.shtml

Online research reports by the Canadian government that review the current literature about what works and what doesn't in the treatment or rehabilitation of criminal offenders.

Yahoo Guide to Corrections and Rehabilitation

http://dir.yahoo.com/society_and_culture/crime/
correction_and_rehabilitation/

A site with listings by topics including prison survival guides, pen pals, correctional education services, and many other issues.

VIOLENT AND SERIAL CRIME

Armed Robbery Page

http://www.armedrobbery.com

A site devoted to the topic of holdups, resistance issues, and employee training at financial institutions.

Assault Prevention Information Network

http://www.jump.net/~judith/APINintro.html

A site that contains information about self-defense resources, martial arts resources, violence in society, and violence prevention.

Child Abuse Prevention Network

http://child-abuse.com

A site providing an almost inexhaustible collection of links on anything to do with child abuse.

Communities against Violence Network

http://www.cavnet.org/

Communities against Violence, or CAVNET, is a good resource site on violence against women, minorities, gays/lesbians, people with disabilities, the crime of stalking, and more.

Domestic Violence Handbook

http://www.domesticviolence.org/

An online resource designed to assist women who are experiencing domestic abuse.

Genesis of a Serial Killer

http://www.jurai.net/~patowic/genesis.html

An online essay about the role of fantasy, addiction, and compulsion in the way some people are brought up which turns them into serial killers, according to this article at least.

Homicide Research Working Group

http://www.icpsr.umich.edu/NACJD/HRWG/

An academic association that publishes the journal, *Homicide Studies*. Only earlier transcripts of their workshops are available online.

Internet Crime Archives

http://www.mayhem.net/Crime/archives.html

A rather shocking site on serial killers, cult killers, and mass murderers.

Justice for All

http://www.jfa.net

A citizens reform group with an excellent collection of links on stalking, gun violence, pro-death penalty resources, and victim's rights.

Men and Women against Domestic Violence

http://www.silcom.com/~paladin/madv/

An informative site with statistics, answers to frequently asked questions, and links to Internet resources on violence against women, including rape.

Minnesota Center against Violence and Abuse

http://www.mincava.umn.edu/

This site has an extensive listing of resources on all kinds of violence against children, women, minorities, and the elderly. It also includes links on gun, school, television, workplace, and gang violence.

National Gay and Lesbian Task Force

http://www.ngltf.org

A site with extensive information on gay-bashing and other hate crimes against sexual minorities.

Partnerships against Violence Network

http://www.pavnet.org/

Partnerships against Violence, or PAVNET, acts as a virtual library or clearinghouse to prevent redundant information on topics related to violence and youth-at-risk.

WHITE COLLAR, ORGANIZED, AND PROPERTY CRIME

Consumer Law Page

http://www.consumerlawpage.com/

This site has resources on negligence, injury, toxins, and corporate crime.

Cybrary: Burglary

http://talkjustice.com/cybrary.asp

A collection of Internet resources on burglary techniques and prevention.

Financial Scandals

http://www.ex.ac.uk/~RDavies/arian/scandals/

An excellent resource site on bank scams, political corruption, and organized crime.

HateWatch

http://hatewatch.org

An extensive resource site with listings of hate groups, church bombings, and bigotry on the Internet.

International Policy Institute for Counter-Terrorism

http://www.ict.org.il/

A think tank's Web site with many online articles and the latest news.

MIT Guide to Lockpicking

http://www.lysator.liu.se/mit-guide/mit-guide.html

The definitive guide on how people break into things.

National Check Fraud Center

http://www.ckfraud.org/

An intelligence collection site on the most common types of financial crimes, including forgery, scams, counterfeiting, and fraud.

Organized Crime Registry

http://members.tripod.com/~orgcrime/index.htm

Coverage of drug cartels and other crime syndicates.

Southern Poverty Law Center

http://www.splcenter.org/

Home of KlanWatch and other militia group monitoring activities.

Web of Justice: Organized Crime Links

http://www.co.pinellas.fl.us/bcc/juscoord/
eorganized.htm

An extensive collection of organized crime links available on the Internet, covers Al Capone to the Yakuza and includes special police units.

E-Journals, Magazines, and Newsletters

APA Journals

http://www.apa.org/journals/

A listing of all journals published by the American Psychological Association.

iSearch: Criminal Justice

Criminal Justice Links: Online Journals and Listservs

http://www.fsu.edu/~crimdo/listserv.html

A mega-list of online journals and discussion lists in criminal justice.

Criminal Justice Policy Review

http://www.chss.iup.edu/cr/cjpr

Only abstracts available online from this journal.

Ethics and Justice

http://www.ethics-justice.org/

Journal for ethics in criminology and criminal Justice with some online articles.

FBI Law Enforcement Bulletin

http://www.fbi.gov/library/leb/leb.htm

This is the online version of a monthly journal by the FBI.

Injustice Studies

http://wolf.its.ilstu.edu/injustice/

Online journal about worldwide atrocities.

International Journal of Drug Testing

http://www.criminology.fsu.edu/journal/

An online journal of research on forensic techniques to detect drugs.

Journal of Credibility Assessment and Witness Psychology

http://truth.boisestate.edu/jcaawp/default.html

An online journal about issues in forensic science and testimony.

Journal of Criminal Justice Ethics

http://www.lib.jjay.cuny.edu/cje/

An online journal site with a collection of links that are labeled as the most useful links in the field. Some of the journal articles are viewable.

Journal of Criminal Justice and Popular Culture

http://www.albany.edu/scj/jcjpc/

An online journal that reviews crime images in the media.

Journal of Online Law

http://www.wm.edu/law/publications/jol/

Online journal devoted to emerging cyberspace law issues.

Journal of Prisoners on Prisoners

http://www.jpp.org/

A rather unique online journal written by prisoners about prisoners.

The Keeper's Voice

http://www.oicj.org/public/

Online newsletter of the International Association of Correctional Officers.

Law and Order Magazine

http://www.lawandordermag.com/

Browsing permitted at this law enforcement magazine site.

Links to Psychological and Social Science Journals

http://www.psywww.com/resource/journals.htm

An index of more than 1,000 links to psychology and social science journal sites.

Online Social Science Journals

http://hypatia.ss.uci.edu/democ/journal.htm

A mega-list of online social science journals, mostly in politics, some in sociology.

Redwood Highway: Electronic Journals

http://www.sonoma.edu/cja/info/infop8.html

A mega-list of electronic journals in criminal justice.

Security Management

http://www.securitymanagement.com/

Online magazine for private security professionals.

Science and Justice

http://www.forensic-science-society.org.uk

Online journal of the Forensic Science Society.

iSearch: Criminal Justice

Scientific Testimony

http://www.scientific.org/

An online journal in forensic science.

Theoretical Criminology

http://www.sagepub.co.uk/journals/details/j0064.html

Some abstracts are available online for this journal.

Western Criminology Review

http://wcr.sonoma.edu/

An excellent online journal with articles on types of crime and justice.

Listservs and Mailing Lists

- CJUST-L: Except for POLICE-L, which is a closed list, this is the world's largest discussion list dedicated to justice issues, where anything goes, except discussion of the right to bear arms. It's hosted by City University of New York's, John Jay College. For information on joining, visit their Web site at **http://listserv.cuny.edu/archives/cjust-l.html.**
- Crime and Clues-L: An open forum for people interested in crime scenes and criminal investigation. For information on joining, visit their Web site at **http://www.dejanews.com/~crimeandclues.**
- CRIT-L: This is the discussion list of the Critical Criminology Division of the American Society of Criminology. It's open to anyone supporting the goals of the division. There's lots of discussion of topical criminal justice issues like the death penalty. For information on joining, visit their Web site at **http://sun.soci.niu.edu/~archives/CRIT-L/crit-l.html.**
- LEANALYST-L: A discussion list for law enforcement analysts, but open to students and anyone interested in analyzing crime. For information on joining, visit their Web site at **http://www.inteltec.com/leanalyst/.**
- NICPUBLIC-L: Official discussion list for the National Institute of Corrections, but open to the public. For information on joining, visit their Web site at **http://www.nicic.org/lists.htm.**
- PRISON-L: This is a discussion list on prison issues and various prison topics hosted by Yale University. To subscribe, send email to listproc@lists.yale.edu with nothing in the subject box and only the words subscribe PRISON-L FirstName LastName in the body of your message.

- Prisons-L: A mailing list for the discussion of issues of concern to correctional officers. For information on joining, visit their Web site at **http://www.onelist.com/subscribe/Prisons.**
- Profiling-L: An open forum for anyone who has an interest in discussing methods and practices of Criminal Profiling. For information on joining, visit their Web site at **http://www.corpus-delicti.com.**
- Rule of Law-L: An open list for people interested in world crime events and the latest justice news from around the world. For information on joining, visit their Web site at **http://www.wjin.net.**
- Treatment Issues in Corrections-L: Run by a correctional employee and open to anybody. For information on joining, visit their Web site at **http://users.downcity.net/~jmm/prison.htm.**

Other Online Resources

Allyn & Bacon Criminal Justice Online

`http://www.ablongman.com/criminaljustice`

This content-rich Web site includes links to a myriad of online resources, such as state-specific web links, media-related links, career information,

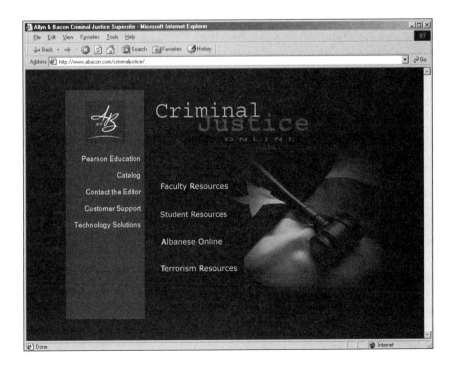

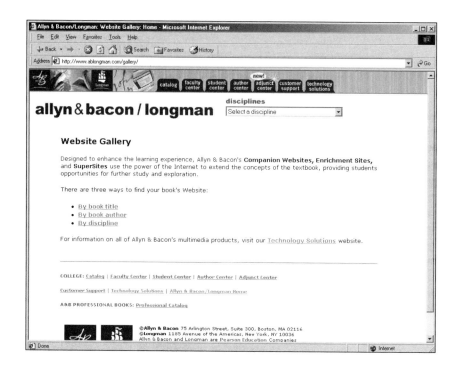

a detailed look at the U.S. Constitution, criminal justice Jeopardy and more.

Allyn & Bacon Criminal Justice Online offers a highly pertinent new section, **Terrorism Resources,** to help students understand the impact of the September 11 attacks upon the criminal justice system. These resources are organized by questions relating to main topics in the study of criminal justice. Resources for investigating the questions include commentary by Allyn and Bacon authors, web links to useful and reliable information sources, and opportunities for students to write their own responses to the questions.

Companion Web Sites

`http://www.abinteractive.com/gallery`

Our Companion Web sites use the Internet to provide you with various opportunities for further study and exploration. The CW offers study content and activities related to the text, as well as an interactive, online study guide. Quizzes containing multiple choice, true/false, and essay questions can be graded instantly, and forwarded to your instructor for recording—all online. For a complete list of titles with a CW, visit **www.abinteractive. com/gallery.**

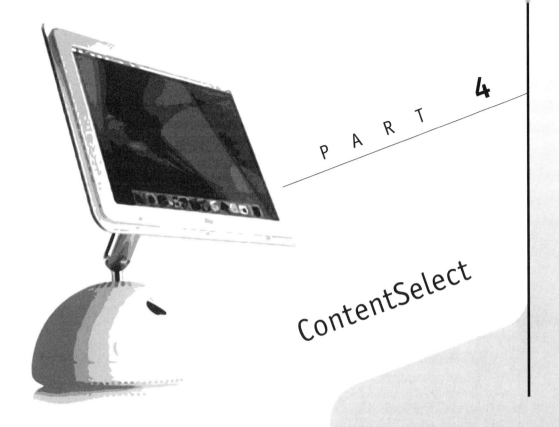

PART 4

ContentSelect

What Is ContentSelect?

ContentSelect for Criminal Justice

`http://www.ablongman.com/contentselect`

Allyn & Bacon and EBSCO Publishing, leaders in the development of electronic journal databases have exclusively collaborated to develop the Criminal Justice ContentSelect Research Database, an online collection of leading scholarly and peer-reviewed journals in the discipline. Students using A&B texts can have free and unlimited access to a customized, searchable collection of 25,000+ discipline-specific articles from top tier academic publications and journals like *The Criminologist, Corrections Today, Crime and Delinquency,* and *Police Quarterly.*

In addition, new features are especially designed to help you with the research process:

- **Start Writing!** With detailed information on the process of writing a research paper, from finding a topic, to gathering data, using the library, using online sources, and more.
- **Internet Research** and **Resource Links** aggregates links to many of the best sites on the Web, providing more tips and best practices to help you use the Web for research.

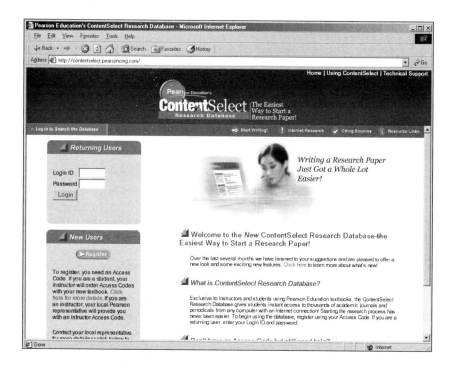

- **Citing Sources.** Featuring excerpts from the best-selling book on research paper, this section helps you understand how and when to cite sources, and includes examples of various citation styles.

How to Use ContentSelect

To begin exploring the great resources available in the ContentSelect Research Database Web site:

Step 1: Go to: **http://www.ablongman.com/contentselect**

Step 2: The resources on the home page will help you start the research and writing process and cite your sources. For invaluable research help,

- Click **Citing Sources** to see how to cite materials with these citation styles: MLA, APA, CMS, and CBE.

- Click **Start Writing!** for step-by-step instructions to help you with the process of writing a research paper.

- Click **Resource Links** and **Internet Research** to link to many of the best sites on the Web with tips to help you efficiently use the Web for research.

Step 3: Register! To start using the ContentSelect Research Database, you will need to register using the access code and instructions located on the inside front cover of this guide. You only need to register once—after you register, you can return to ContentSelect at any time, and log in using your personal login name and password.

Step 4: Log in! Type in your login name and password in the spaces provided to access ContentSelect. Then click through the pages to enter the research database, and see the list of disciplines. You can search for articles within a single discipline, or select as many disciplines as you want! To see the list of journals included in any database, just click the "**complete title list**" link located next to each discipline—check back often, as this list will grow throughout the year!

Step 5: To begin your search, simply select your discipline(s), and **click "Enter"** to begin your search. For tips and detailed search instructions, please visit the "ContentSelect Search Tips" section included in this guide.

For more help, and search tips, click the Online Help button on the right side of your screen.

Go to **www.ablongman.com/contentselect** now, to discover the easiest way to start a research paper!

ContentSelect Search Tips

Searching for articles in ContentSelect is easy! Here are some tips to help you find articles for your research paper.

Tip 1: **Select a discipline.** When you first enter the ContentSelect Research Database, you will see a list of disciplines. To search within a single discipline, click the name of the discipline. To search in more than one discipline, click the box next to each discipline and click the **ENTER** button.

Basic Search

The following tips will help you with a Basic Search.

iSearch: Criminal Justice

Tip 2: **Basic Search.** After you select your discipline(s), you will go to the Basic Search Window. Basic Search lets you search for articles using a variety of methods. You can select from: Standard Search, Match All Words, Match Any Words, or Match Exact Phrase. For more information on these options, click the <u>Search Tips</u> link at any time!

Tip 3: **Using AND, OR, and NOT** to help you search. In Standard Search, you can use AND, OR and NOT to create a very broad or very narrow search:

- **AND** searches for articles containing all of the words. For example, typing **education AND technology** will search for articles that contain **both** education AND technology.

- **OR** searches for articles that contains at least one of the terms. For example, searching for **education OR technology** will find articles that contain either education OR technology.

- **NOT** excludes words so that the articles will not include the word that follows "NOT." For example, searching for **education NOT technology** will find articles that contain the term education but NOT the term technology.

Tip 4: **Using Match All Words.** When you select the Match All Words option, you do not need to use the word AND—you will automatically search for articles that only contain all of the words. The order of the search words entered in does not matter. For example, typing **education technology** will search for articles that contain **both** education AND technology.

Tip 5: **Using Match Any Words.** After selecting the "Match Any Words" option, type words, a phrase, or a sentence in the window. ContentSelect will search for articles that contain any of the terms you typed (but will not search for words such as **in** and **the**). For example, type **rising medical costs in the United States** to find articles that contain *rising, medical, costs, United,* or *States.* To limit your search to find articles that contain exact terms, use *quotation marks*—for example, typing "United States" will only search for articles containing "United States."

Tip 6: **Using Match Exact Phrase.** Select this option to find articles containing an exact phrase. ContentSelect will search for articles that include all the words you entered, exactly as you entered them. For example, type **rising medical costs in the United States** to find articles that contain the exact phrase "rising medical costs in the United States."

Guided Search

The following tips will help you with a Guided Search.

Tip 7: To switch to a Guided Search, click the **Guided Search** tab on the navigation bar, just under the EBSCO Host logo. The *Guided Search Window* helps you focus your search using multiple text boxes, Boolean operators (AND, OR, and NOT), and various search options.

To create a search:

- Type the words you want to search for in the Find field.

- Select a field from the drop-down list. For example: AU-Author will search for an author. For more information on fields, click Search Tips.

- Enter additional search terms in the text boxes (optional), and select *and, or, not* to connect multiple search terms (see Tip 3 for information on *and, or,* and *not*).

- Click **Search.**

Expert Search

The following tips will help you with an Expert Search.

Tip 8: To switch to an Expert Search, click the **Expert Search** tab on the navigation bar, just under the EBSCO Host logo. The *Expert Search Window* uses your keywords and search history search for articles. Please note, searches run from the Basic or Guided Search Windows are not saved to the History File used by the Expert Search Window—only Expert Searches are saved in the history.

Tip 9: Expert Searches use **Limiters** and **Field Codes** to help you search for articles. For more information on Limiters and Field Codes, click Search Tips.

Explore all the search options available in ContentSelect! For more information and tips, click the Online Help button, located on the right side of every page.

iSearch: Criminal Justice

Your Own Private Glossary

The Glossary in this book contains reference terms you'll find useful as you get started on the Internet. After a while, however, you'll find yourself running across abbreviations, acronyms, and buzzwords whose definitions will make more sense to you once you're no longer a novice (or "newbie"). That's the time to build a glossary of your own. For now, the Webopedia gives you a place to start.

alias   A simple email address that can be used in place of a more complex one.

AVI   Audio Video Interleave. A video compression standard developed for use with Microsoft Windows. Video clips on the World Wide Web are usually available in both AVI and QuickTime formats.

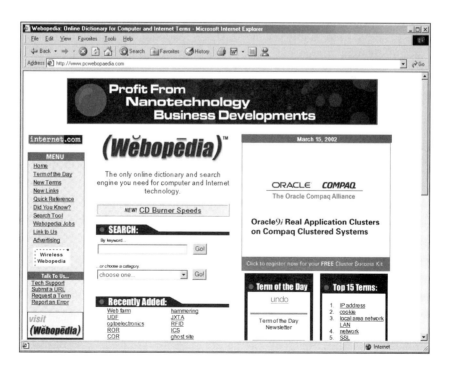

bandwidth   Internet parlance for capacity to carry or transfer information such as email and Web pages.

browser   The computer program that lets you view the contents of Web sites.

client   A program that runs on your personal computer and supplies you with Internet services, such as getting your mail.

cyberspace   The whole universe of information that is available from computer networks. The term was coined by science fiction writer William Gibson in his novel *Neuromancer,* published in 1984.

DNS   See *domain name server.*

domain   A group of computers administered as a single unit, typically belonging to a single organization such as a university or corporation.

domain name   A name that identifies one or more computers belonging to a single domain. For example, "apple.com".

domain name server   A computer that converts domain names into the numeric addresses used on the Internet.

download   Copying a file from another computer to your computer over the Internet.

email   Electronic mail.

emoticon   A guide to the writer's feelings, represented by typed characters, such as the Smiley :-). Helps readers understand the emotions underlying a written message.

FAQs   Frequently Asked Questions

flame   A rude or derogatory message directed as a personal attack against an individual or group.

flame war   An exchange of flames (see above).

ftp   File Transfer Protocol, a method of moving files from one computer to another over the Internet.

home page   A page on the World Wide Web that acts as a starting point for information about a person or organization.

hypertext   Text that contains embedded *links* to other pages of text. Hypertext enables the reader to navigate between pages of related information by following links in the text.

LAN   Local Area Network. A computer network that is located in a concentrated area, such as offices within a building.

iSearch: Criminal Justice

link   A reference to a location on the Web that is embedded in the text of the Web page. Links are usually highlighted with a different color or underlined to make them easily visible.

listserv   Strictly speaking, a computer program that administers electronic mailing lists, but also used to denote such lists or discussion groups, as in "the writer's listserv."

lurker   A passive reader of an Internet *newsgroup* or *listserv*. A lurker reads messages, but does not participate in the discussion by posting or responding to messages.

mailing list   A subject-specific automated email system. Users subscribe and receive email from other users about the subject of the list.

modem   A device for connecting two computers over a telephone line.

newbie   A new user of the Internet.

newsgroup   A discussion forum in which all participants can read all messages and public replies between the participants.

plug-in   A third-party software program that will lend a Web browser (Netscape, Internet Explorer, etc.) additional features.

quoted   Text in an email message or newsgroup posting that has been set off by the use of vertical bars or > characters in the left-hand margin.

search engine   A computer program that will locate Web sites or files based on specified criteria.

secure   A Web page whose contents are encrypted when sending or receiving information.

server   A computer program that moves information on request, such as a Web server that sends pages to your browser.

Smiley   See *emoticon*.

snail mail   Mail sent the old fashioned way: Write a letter, put it in an envelope, stick on a stamp, and drop it in the mailbox.

spam   Spam is to the Internet as unsolicited junk mail is to the postal system.

URL   Uniform Resource Locator: The notation for specifying addresses on the World Wide Web (e.g. http://www.abacon.com or ftp://ftp. abacon.com).

Usenet   The section of the Internet devoted to *newsgroups*.

iSearch: Criminal Justice

Web browser   A program used to navigate and access information on the World Wide Web. Web browsers convert html coding into a display of pictures, sound, and words.

Web page   All the text, graphics, pictures, and so forth, denoted by a single URL beginning with the identifier "http://".

Web site   A collection of World Wide Web pages, usually consisting of a home page and several other linked pages.